MW00438778

WINNING YOUR SPIRITUAL BATTLES

Winning Your Spiritual Battles

How to Use the Full Armor of God

GARY D. KINNAMAN

SERVANT PUBLICATIONS
ANN ARBOR, MICHIGAN

Copyright 2003 by Gary Kinnaman
All rights reserved.

Vine Books is an imprint of Servant Publications especially designed to serve evangelical Christians.

Servant Mission Statement

We are dedicated to publishing books that spread the gospel of Jesus Christ, help Christians to live in accordance with that gospel, promote renewal in the church, and bear witness to Christian unity.

Unless otherwise indicated, Scripture quotations are from the HOLY BIBLE, NEW INTERNATIONAL VERSION®. Copyright 1973, 1978, 1984 by International Bible Society. Used by permission of Zondervan Publishing House. All rights reserved. Quotations marked AMPLIFIED are from the Amplified Bible, New Testament © The Lockman Foundation, Old Testament © Zondervan. Quotations marked EMPHASIZED are from the Emphasized Bible, © Joseph Bryant Rotherham, Kregal Publishers. Quotations marked KJV are from the King James Version of the Bible. Quotations marked THE MESSAGE are from *The Message,* © by Eugene H. Peterson. Quotations marked NEB are from The New English Bible, © The Delegates of the Oxford University Press and the Syndics of Cambridge University Press. Quotations marked NASB are from the New American Standard Bible © The Lockman Foundation. Quotations marked NKJV are from the New King James Version of the Bible © Thomas Nelson, Inc., Publishers. Italics in Scripture quotes have been added by the author.

Published by Servant Publications
P.O. Box 8617
Ann Arbor, Michigan 48107
www.servantpub.com

Cover design: Steve Eames

03 04 05 06 10 9 8 7 6 5 4 3 2 1

Printed in the United States of America
ISBN 1-56955-373-4

Library of Congress Cataloging-in-Publication Data

Kinnaman, Gary.
  Winning your spiritual battles : how to use the full armor of God /
Gary D. Kinnaman.
      p. cm.
Includes bibliographical references and index.
  ISBN 1-56955-373-4 (alk. paper)
  1. Spiritual warfare. I. Title.
BV4509.5.K485 2003
245'.4--dc21
                                        2003007194

Contents

ONE

A Reality Check

This is for keeps, a life-or-death fight to the finish against the Devil and all his angels.

EPHESIANS 6:12, THE MESSAGE

Karl and his wife, Dee, were suddenly awakened in the middle of the night.

BANG! WHAP! BANG!

"What was *that?*" Karl mumbled. Someone was pounding violently on their door. "Call 911," he urged his wife in a raspy whisper, then felt his way to the front of the house.

WHAP! WHAP! BANG! The battering continued.

Karl reached the door and shouted, *"What do you want?!"*

"Someone broke the windshield of my car," came the frenzied reply. "They're in this house, *AND I'M GONNA KILL 'EM!"*

And then, as Karl later told me, it occurred to him to pray. Remember that little statement: *It occurred to him to pray.* So assertively, boldly, Karl shouted to God, "In the name of Jesus I rebuke the spirit in the man on the other side of my door. Deliver us from this evil!"

"Within seconds of praying," he reported, "the enraged man vanished from my front porch.

"I'm telling you this," he confessed, "not just to let you know about how God worked a miracle in our behalf, but also to admit how ashamed I am that it took me so long to think about praying. Prayer was *not* my first response. I feel just terrible that I didn't pray *first*." It

7

was an indictment, he felt, of the superficiality of his relationship with God.

Ironically, if you knew Karl, you'd have to say he is one of the most godly people you'll ever meet. No spiritual slouch, Karl was serving as chairman of our board of elders.

What's Up With That?

Take a long hard look at the Bible verse right there at the beginning of this chapter: *This is for keeps*. And ponder this: *It's a life-or-death fight to the finish against the Devil and all his angels*. Do we *really* believe this? Does my friend Karl? We say we do, but if this is in fact our reality, then why don't we pray more, pray longer, pray sooner?

In the week immediately after the 9-11 attacks on America, our weekend services and special prayer events at Word of Grace Church in Mesa, Arizona, were jammed with over nine thousand people, twice as many as normally attend on the weekends. Why? Because for a brief month or so Americans really believed that our world is in a life-or-death fight to the finish.

But a year later, when we call for a day of prayer and fasting? Of the several thousand adults who attend on the weekend, only several hundred show up for our special prayer service on Tuesday night. The reason? We've been lulled by our comfortable world into thinking that life is *not* an intense spiritual battle. And if life does get intense, it "occurs to us to pray" only after we've exhausted every natural option.

Ask yourself, "What's the reality, the worldview of Christians I know? What's my reference point for understanding what happens in my life? What's my reality? Do I *really* live my life as if every day is 'a life-or-death fight to the finish against the Devil and all his angels'?"

Fearful in Cali

I've had the privilege of traveling to some of the most extraordinary places in the world, where people in the worst imaginable conditions have the most incredible faith. Take, for example, Cali, Colombia, perhaps the most violent city in the world. Ravaged by drug wars, probably no urban area on the planet has a higher murder rate.

I knew that, but I agreed to go there to speak at a conference for Christian leaders. Yes, "it occurred to me to pray." I was apprehensive about going, especially after calling the U.S. State Department's twenty-four-hour travel advisory for Colombia. It warned Americans to avoid travel to that part of the world. And then, just a couple weeks before our departure, the son of one of the gentlemen accompanying me on the trip, Harold Christ, sent his father a copy of a front-page article in the *Atlanta Constitution* about revolution and violence in Colombia. Strike two.

I still have a hard time believing what happened next. About a week before our trip, Harold was peacefully drinking an early morning cup of coffee in an outdoor café when someone called him on his cell phone. An acquaintance who works for the U.S. State Department heard Harold was traveling to Colombia and called to persuade him not to go.

"Well," Harold told him reluctantly, "I'm going with my pastor, and we all feel like this is something God is leading us to do."

"OK," replied his friend, "but let me make one more call for you. I know someone who works for the CIA in Mexico City."

Ten minutes later Harold's phone rang again. "It's me. Listen, I spoke with my contact in Mexico, and he told me in no uncertain terms (he actually used profanity), 'Tell your friend *to stay out of Colombia.*'"

At that precise moment a pigeon rushed by Harold's face and smashed into the heavy, dark window next to his table. Fluttering to the ground, the bird staggered under Harold's chair. Thinking mostly about the phone call, Harold paid no attention to the pigeon until the man at the next table exclaimed, "Look at that!"

"Right there," Harold told me, "right under my chair, was that bird, dead. In a pool of blood."

Yes, a pool of blood. Strike three.

Of course, Harold called me *immediately* to tell me what had happened. We prayed, and I assured him that I would have my pastors' covenant group pray with me about whether or not God was trying to warn us.

Well, bless my dear pastor friends! Not one of them felt we should cancel the trip! So like Queen Esther of old, I said to myself, "If I perish, I perish!"

Dangerous Christians

Obviously I've lived to tell the story. Not once did any of our ministry team feel any sense of danger whatsoever during our short week in Cali. Well, except for one time.

We were being escorted to a prayer meeting like none I'd ever seen. A *vigilia*, or prayer vigil, the event was planned for a huge soccer stadium seating perhaps fifty to sixty thousand people. By the time we arrived, *every seat was taken,* and an estimated ten thousand rowdy Christians were trying to get in! Being escorted through that crushing crowd and squeezed through a narrow, rusty chain-link gate that nearly tore the buttons from my shirt comprised my only moment of real fear. I thought I was going to die at a prayer meeting!

Imagine having to turn away ten thousand people from an all-night prayer meeting! And did they go home? Are you kidding? Those masses of people stayed right there outside the stadium, praying all night.

Here's a little quiz about world Christianity: Do you think sixty to seventy thousand people praying all night believe that it's "for keeps, a life-or-death fight to the finish against the Devil and all his angels"? It is, you know. The prayer movement in Cali began, in fact, in a pool of blood, when Pastor Julio Ruibal was shot dead on the sidewalk on his way to a pastors' prayer meeting.

Two years ago I was in Abuja, the capital of Nigeria. A city of contrasts, it boasts some of the most modern, beautiful buildings in Africa and yet, like every sub-Saharan urban area, is home to tens of thousands of people living in wretched conditions.

Led by Ina and Sarah Omakwu, graduates of Regent University in Virginia Beach, Family Love Center is a church that's grown in just a few years to a weekend attendance of six thousand, 40 percent of whom are unemployed. Without borrowing a cent and with very little financial help from the outside world, this congregation built a functional but striking multimillion-dollar worship center.

Pastor Ina and his wife live in one of the better parts of the city, in a cluster of modest homes—we would consider them lower-middle-class—each of which is protected by a walled enclosure. Nasty shards of broken glass are set in concrete along the tops of the walls to discourage intruders. Like many homeowners in the area, Pastor Ina has two private security guards standing at his driveway entrance twenty-four hours a day.

Never once have I heard Pastor Ina say, "I think this is something we should pray about," because he prays about *everything*. Immediately! His first response in every situation is prayer, because he knows that it's "for keeps, a life-or-death fight to the finish against the Devil and all his angels."

Praying, Naturally

Why does prayer come so "naturally" to global Christians? There are at least two reasons. First, their lives are more desperate. For most Christians outside the United States and Canada, clinging to God is, literally, a matter of life or death. Second, in most places in Asia, Africa, and Latin America, people do not believe in the popular but artificial Western distinction between "the natural" and "the supernatural." All of life—natural and supernatural—is integrated.

In other words, most of the people in our world absolutely believe that the spiritual realm interfaces daily with every little thing in their lives. What is convicting for North Americans is that this was the worldview of the writers of the Bible. It's why the apostle Paul could declare without apology or explanation, "This is for keeps, a life-or-death fight to the finish against the Devil and all his angels."

In an article titled "Shifting Worldviews, Sifting Attitudes," Fuller Seminary professor and prolific author Charles Kraft describes how his failures in the mission field led him to spiritual renewal and a healing ministry.

> [My wife and I] had been brought up as "typical" evangelicals....
> [We] completed seminary and a year of specialized mission studies and were off to Nigeria to serve as pioneer church and language/Bible translation missionaries.... We went out well-trained in biblical studies, anthropology and linguistics.
>
> We were well-prepared—except, as it turned out, in the area the Nigerians considered the most important: their relationship with the spirit world. These spirits, they told me, cause disease, accidents and death, hinder fertility of people, animals and fields, bring drought, destroy relationships, and harass the innocent.

But I could not help these people, for I was just plain ignorant in this area.[1]

So what do you believe? That Nigerians are superstitious? If you do, then you will probably have difficulty accepting Ephesians 6:12 literally. The Nigerians certainly accept it—and the Colombians! I have seen that! And when I come back home to America, I see how everyone is so comfortable, so indifferent.

Oh, I don't want to downplay the enormous social problems we are facing in America—the epidemics of divorce, teen suicide, AIDS, urban poverty. Nor dare I discount the passionate prayer of thousands of devoted Christians in cities across America. But by and large, other parts of the Christian world are much more realistic about the spiritual causes of broken lives and a troubled world.

The New Christendom

In a landmark book, *The Next Christendom,* historian and scholar Philip Jenkins writes about the coming of global Christianity. The jacket cover states:

In looking back over the enormous changes wrought by the Twentieth Century, Western observers may have missed the most dramatic revolution of all. While secular movements like communism, feminism, and environmentalism have gotten the lion's share of our attention, the explosive southward expansion of Christianity in Africa, Asia, and Latin America has barely registered on Western consciousness.

What does Jenkins tell us about the uniqueness of "the new Christendom"?

If there is a single key area of faith and practice that divides Northern [Hemisphere] and Southern [Hemisphere] Christians, it is this matter of spiritual forces and their effects on the everyday human world. This issue goes to the heart of cultural definition and worldviews. In traditional African society [for example], various forms of divination were used to seek out the cause of evil, and to identify the wrongdoer as an essential first step toward neutralizing his or her evil powers. At every stage, this scheme of explanations offended the sensibilities of European missionaries, who saw themselves in a heroic struggle against the evils of superstition, fatalism, and witchcraft. How could churches possibly accept such ideas?

... For African Christians, one of the most potent passages of the New Testament is found in the letter to the Ephesians, in which Paul declares that "our struggle is not against flesh and blood."... However superstitious and irrelevant it appears to mainstream Northern Christians, the passage makes wonderful sense in most of Africa, as it does for believers in Latin America or East Asia.[2]

In a cover article in *The Atlantic Monthly,* Jenkins adds "Worldwide, Christianity is actually moving toward supernaturalism ... and in many ways toward the ancient worldview expressed in the New Testament: a vision of Jesus as the embodiment of divine power, who overcomes the evil forces that inflict calamity and sickness upon the human race."[3]

Highly respected theologian Clinton Arnold, of Talbot Seminary in California, identified this same crucial issue in his book *Powers of*

Darkness, a study of spiritual warfare based on the writings of Paul.

The Western worldview does not represent everyone in the West. Nevertheless, *an antisupernatural bias* still characterizes the academic community in the West and perhaps also a majority of the populous, although change is on the horizon.... What I am suggesting is that we engage in a critical re-evaluation of our Western worldview on one important issue—the actual existence of good and evil spirits.... We must ... strive toward making this as important a part of our worldview as it was for Paul. *The powers of darkness are real, we need to be conscious of their influence, and we need to respond to them appropriately.*[4]

In summary, then, the prayer and spiritual life of many Christians in North America is assaulted by two subtle but powerful forces. The first is a pervasive antisupernatural bias—that is, people just don't believe in miracles. As best-selling author and researcher of world spirituality George Otis observes, "The worldview of most non-Westerners is three-tiered: on the top is the cosmic, transcendental world; in the middle are supernatural forces on the earth; and on the bottom rests the empirical world of our senses. The unique tendency of Western society has been to ignore the middle zone."

The second major challenge for us living in the West is our busy life full of happy distractions, from malls to restaurants, from multiplex theaters to the Internet, from inexpensive air travel to hundreds of channels on cable television. I'll never forget the comment of a spiritually rich Chinese Christian leader, just two weeks out of China. Speaking to a group of American Christian leaders, he said, "I can see it is very difficult to be a Christian in America, because you have so many distractions."

Back to the Bible

So where do we go from here? Right back to the Bible: "This is for keeps, a life-or-death fight to the finish against the Devil and all his angels." We have to believe it. We have to live and pray as if we believe it. We must pray that God would open our eyes to the reality, influence, and power of the spiritual realm.

Before taking a close look at the armor of God, the heart and soul of this book, we must embark on a journey of *re*discovery of the spiritual realm. What, specifically, are some things the Bible reveals about the spiritual dimension? According to Ephesians 6:10, we have to begin by going back to the basics: *Put God first.* Paul says as he prepares to end his Letter to the Ephesians, "Be strong in the Lord and in his mighty power."

Whatever life brings, whatever happens, you have to center your life in God, because life is fundamentally spiritual. The familiar term *godless* doesn't just mean the worst a person can be. *Godless* in the Bible means living your life as if there is no God, as if heaven and hell don't exist.

Let's go back to my friend Karl, who called the police first, reasoned with an unreasonable man second, and prayed third. Not that it was wrong for Karl's wife to dial 911! But not to pray *first* in any situation is godless. It is a response of spiritual superficiality. It shows that we do not think that we are *really* in a life-or-death fight to the finish.

Paul writes that "though we live in the world, we do not wage war as the world does" (2 Corinthians 10:3). I take this to mean that we don't use a natural view of things to understand life and take on its problems. "The weapons we fight with," he adds, "are not the weapons of the world" (verse 4a). In other words, we don't solve our problems the way the world does, godlessly. "The fear of the Lord is the beginning of wisdom," which means, literally, "life skill" in the ancient Hebrew text of Proverbs 9:10. In contrast to the world's way of looking at life and solving its problems, we fight with the weapons of the Spirit, which have "divine power to demolish strongholds" (2 Corinthians 10:4a).

People Problems Aren't What You Think

No, I'm not suggesting that Christians abandon practical life skills! But I am convinced that we must be God-minded in *everything* we do. This means we will, indeed, recognize the reality and power of the spiritual dimension.

Take, for example, family issues and relationships in the workplace. Probably 90 percent of all the flesh and blood in your life is right there. And there are any number of things we can learn about conflict resolution, listening skills, forgiveness, and empathy to help us relate to one another in more godly ways. The fruit of the Spirit in Galatians 5:22-23, for example, is a list of essential virtues that will put us in good standing in just about every relationship.

But is that all we need to know? Will life work for us if we just work harder on life? If Paul's perspective on spiritual conflict in Ephesians is to be taken seriously, if our struggle is *not with flesh and blood,* then there must be more to problems at home and work than what first meets the eye.

If you have a *New International Version* Bible, look at Ephesians 5. What's the editor's heading right after 5:21? "Wives and husbands." And the next heading? "Parents and children." And the next? "Slaves and masters," or to bring it into the twenty-first century, employees and employers.

Yes, and after all that practical teaching on the two principal arenas of life—home and work—Paul says, "Therefore, be strong in the Lord," and "put on the full armor of God." In other words, all the extraordinary, other-worldly things he is about to teach us about spiritual warfare and the armor of God are right there in the context of ordinary, this-worldly home and work!

So be strong in the Lord, and put on the whole armor of God, because this life-or-death struggle is *not* with the spouse, or the kids, or the in-laws, or the boss, or that person you have to work with. We don't really have people problems! Our struggles are, at their core, spiritual. *Every little thing in life interfaces with the spiritual realm.* Again, this is why we can't approach life as the world does—godlessly ignorant of the spiritual realm.

It's a serious matter, so serious that Paul chose to use a Greek term for "the struggle" that suggests the gladiatorial contests of ancient Rome. Did you see *Gladiator?* Rated "R" for traumatic violence, it's as brutal a movie as you'll ever see. I still recommend it for adults, though, because it's a vivid re-creation of Paul's world.

Spend an evening with that movie, and you'll understand with painful clarity what Paul meant when he said, "This is for keeps, a life-or-death fight to the finish." In the Roman Colosseum the winning team didn't just score more points. They won by ruthlessly killing everyone on the other side. Everyone on the losing team died in a savage "fight to the finish."

Yes, spiritual warfare is that serious, and that's why the armor of God is so necessary.

Be Able to Stand

Fortunately, though, not every problem in life is specifically demonic, and not every day is full of terrible evil. Spiritual implications to everything? Yes. Direct interference of the devil in everything? No. Paul writes, "Put on the full armor of God, so that *when the day of evil comes*, you may be able to stand" (Ephesians 6:13). In other words, putting on the armor of God is like saving money for that proverbial rainy day, or working out at the gym to extend the life of your cardiovascular system. The armor of God gets us ready for when the day of evil comes.

Be alert to the possibility of spiritual attack, "for your enemy the devil prowls about as a roaring lion, looking for someone to devour" (1 Peter 2:8). Be vigilant, but don't drive yourself crazy. If the devil can't keep you from believing he's real, he'll do everything possible to get you to believe he's personally responsible for every bad thing in your life, from family problems to flat tires. Not every day is the day of evil!

Finally, no matter what life brings or how long the trial lasts, never get discouraged, and never give up. I love this: "Put on the full armor of God, so that when the day of evil comes, you may be able to *stand your ground*, and after you have done everything, *to stand. Stand firm then*" (Ephesians 6:13-14).

In what is undoubtedly the most gripping scene in *Gladiator*, the hero, Maximus, is sent into the arena with a handful of other gladiators to face a small army of well-equipped charioteers. The hero has little chance to survive, but as a former military commander, he demands of the other gladiators that they stand together. "If they separate us," he reminds them as the fearsome chariots circle their little band of warriors, "we will all die."

As recently as 150 years ago, in the bloody American Civil War, fighting men stood shoulder to shoulder against a barrage of bullets. If one person bolted, the entire army could lose the field of battle. For everyone to stand together, rank upon rank, no matter what the cost—even if it meant death—was essential.

I've never been in combat, but I can only imagine that standing in a line of battle, repelling one attack after another, would be a terrible test of a man's will and soul. J.B. Phillips, in his *New Testament in Modern English*, translates Ephesians 6:14, "Even when you have fought to a standstill you may still stand your ground." I've said it this way, "When everything is at a standstill, stand still!" Never give in, and never give up the fight.

But don't do it naked!

Stand firm then, with the belt of truth buckled around your waist, with the breastplate of righteousness in place, and with your feet fitted with the readiness that comes from the gospel of peace. In addition to all this, take up the shield of faith, with which you can extinguish all the flaming arrows of the evil one. Take the helmet of salvation and the sword of the Spirit, which is the word of God.

EPHESIANS 6:14-17

TWO

Resisting the Devil

Resist the devil, and he will flee from you.

JAMES 4:7

Life is a spiritual battle. "Our struggle is not against flesh and blood, but against the powers of this dark world and against the spiritual forces of evil in the heavenly realms" (Ephesians 6:12).

If this is true—and we have seen that it is—then the development of our spiritual sensitivity and power is absolutely necessary. Unfortunately, there is only one way for this to happen: experience. The troubles of life are actually opportunities to build up our faith and strengthen our relationship with God. They make us more skilled and effective soldiers of the kingdom.

Faith comes by hearing the Word of God (Romans 10:17), but faith does not grow without exercise. Reading the Bible without practicing its principles in the arena of life is like reading tennis magazines without ever walking onto a court. All the training videos in the world will never make you a tennis player. Reading about war does not make you a soldier, but basic training and combat will!

Romans 5:3-4 unfolds the process of spiritual development: "We rejoice in our sufferings." Why? "Because we know that suffering produces perseverance; perseverance [produces] character; and character [produces] hope." The apostle Paul almost seemed to welcome trouble, not because trouble is pleasant but because it gave him an opportunity to grow in his faith: "Therefore I will boast all the more gladly about my weaknesses, so that Christ's power may rest on me. That is why, for Christ's sake, I delight in weaknesses, in insults, in hardships, in persecutions, in difficulties. For when I am weak, then I am strong" (2 Corinthians 12:9-10).

James had the same unusual way of looking at life: "Consider it pure joy, my brothers, whenever you face trials of many kinds." Why? "Because you know that the testing of your faith develops perseverance" (James 1:2-3).

Resistance Means You Will Get Stronger

Bodybuilding is based on the principle of resistance: the more weight, the more the resistance; and the more the resistance, the more the muscles develop. Competition weight lifters welcome resistance. In fact, they keep increasing it to push their strength to the limit.

Respect Satan's power, but don't fear it. Accept it as a challenge to the practice of your faith. Spiritual resistance is spiritual bodybuilding.

A few years ago my wife and I returned to Kansas for our college reunion. We had not been on the campus for decades, but the memories were as fresh as the sunrise that morning. After walking around the campus, I wanted to spend a few moments on the soccer field where I had practiced and played for two years. Do you know what I remembered the most? The agony of the first week of practice and the painful walk from the showers in the gym to the student union building for the evening meal.

Exercise does not create new muscles; it lets you discover and strengthen the ones you have. Trouble in life doesn't give you faith. Only Jesus can do that. But life's battles have the potential of increasing your spiritual strength, provided you use them to exercise your faith. With every problem there is a solution. With every temptation God will provide a way of escape. You can think of life as either full of problems or full of opportunities.

The author of Hebrews saw value in the exercise and pain of life. He wrote, "No discipline seems pleasant at the time, but painful. Later on, however, it produces a harvest of righteousness and peace for those who have been trained [exercised] by it" (Hebrews 12:11). The weights of life will either crush you or exercise you. The devil, your opponent, will either destroy you or test your spiritual skills. If you give in to the pain and give up, he will devour you. Resist him and he will flee from you.

Resistance Means "to Stand Against"

The Greek term translated "resist" in James 4:7 and 1 Peter 5:9, where we are told to resist the devil, is *anthistemi* (or *antihistemi*), which means literally "to stand against." Obviously, it is the term from which we derive our English word *antihistamine*. An antihistamine is a medication that helps you "stand against" the symptoms of sinus allergies or the common cold.

The protests in Tianemen Square in Beijing, China, gave the world a powerful image of resistance. How can we forget the photo of the young Chinese man standing rigid in front of an army tank, its ugly gun barrel aimed directly at his head. Resistance! Freedom fighters refuse to say *die*, even in the face of insurmountable odds.

The armor of God, described in Ephesians 6, and which we will study in the next few chapters, is our best means of resistance. In fact, resistance to spiritual darkness is high when you are wearing the whole armor of God. On the other hand, standing against the devil is impossible when you are not wearing it.

Resisting the Devil and Restraining Yourself

Another word for *resist* is *restrain,* and a synonym of *restrain* is *bind.* When you resist the devil you restrain him, and when you restrain him you bind him. You bind the devil with your actions, not just your words.

Resisting the devil, then, begins with restraining yourself. Peter teaches us that self-control is a prerequisite for resisting the devil: "Be self controlled and alert. Your enemy the devil prowls around like a roaring lion looking for someone to devour" (1 Peter 5:8). In other words, you cannot resist the devil effectively if you can't rule yourself.

Hapuna Beach is one of the largest and most popular strands of sand on the Kona Coast of Hawaii's Big Island. A large sign confronts you as you walk toward the ocean: "Warning. Dangerous currents. If you get caught in the current, *don't panic.* Let the current carry you out to sea. It will weaken, and you will be able to swim back to shore."

Life is full of currents that carry us places we really don't want to go. Most are circumstantial; some are spiritual. Often it is not possible to overcome the current immediately, and the most effective resistance is just keeping our composure. Self-control alone can garner great spiritual victories.

The opposite of self-control is panic. I was once within a few breaths of drowning. Snorkeling is really a safe and simple sport. Elderly people do it; children do it. But one time my friend Tim wanted us to swim a fair distance into the open ocean, beyond the shelter of a rocky cove. He also convinced me that I could not really enjoy myself snorkeling unless I wore a weight belt to make me less buoyant, in the event I decided to dive.

I had more than I was prepared to handle: deep water, ocean swells, a leaky face mask, and the weight belt dragging me down. I started gulping for air as panic set in. My only hope was to cling to a jagged rock, made even more dangerous by an encrustation of barnacles and sea urchins.

I decided in a flash to trade oblivion in the blue Pacific for a painful climb on the rocks. My friend screamed at me, "Don't do it!" But I had no choice. I knew I had to regain my composure. I did, and I am alive to tell the story, albeit with the memory of bleeding shins stained purple by sea urchin spines.

Winning life's battles often requires a cool head. And if you want the upper hand over the dominion of darkness, be sober and vigilant. Be watchful and alert. Resist the devil by restraining yourself.

Paul suggests this when he writes, "Don't let the sun go down on your anger." In other words, don't let your emotions get the best of you. "And do not give the devil a foothold" (Ephesians 4:26-27).

Resisting the Devil, Not People

There is a fine line between resisting the devil, who frequently works through other people, and resisting the people who are his unwitting instruments. In Matthew 5:39 Jesus cautions us, "Do not resist [*anti-histemi*] an evil person."

When I first discovered this reference in the context of my study of *resist*, it puzzled me. Then I realized that Jesus is simply telling us, "Don't stand up for yourself all the time. Let God fight your battles. God alone is your defense against the devil and the people he influences for evil."

Sometimes resistance means "going with the flow" without losing an ounce of faith that God is ultimately going to win the battle for you. Resisting and resting seem contradictory, but resisting the devil and resting in God go hand in hand. Sometimes the best resistance is no resistance.

Jesus is our example: "Christ suffered for you, leaving you an example, that you should follow in his steps. 'He committed no sin, and no deceit was found in his mouth.' When they hurled their insults at him, he did not retaliate. [He restrained Himself, but He did not cave in to the pressure.] Instead [and this is the key], he entrusted himself to him who judges justly" (1 Peter 2:21-23). The kingdom must be taken by force, but the force is the cross—renouncing self—trust, and clinging to God. Resist the devil, but be kind to people, even if they are your enemies (Matthew 5:44).

Putting on the Armor

Spiritual warfare is a difficult and demanding business. Our adversary is the second most powerful being in the universe. He is highly intelligent, is clever beyond measure, and cannot be outwitted. The only effective spiritual antihistamine, then, is the armor of God.

"Finally, be strong in the Lord and in his mighty power. Put on the armor of God so that you can take your stand against the devil's schemes" (Ephesians 6:10-11). The armor of God is "his mighty power."

Only by the power of God and our authority in Jesus are we able to resist and overcome the dominion of darkness. The mountains of life and the strongholds of our spiritual enemies are removed "not by [human] might nor by [human] power, but by my Spirit, says the Lord Almighty" (Zechariah 4:6).

Even a book like this on strategies for spiritual warfare will not give you answers to all the questions you might have about spiritual warfare. In fact, Satan is so astute that the Bible does not present a single, fail-safe plan against him. It warns us about the devi's schemes. It tells us to submit to God. The Bible commands us to be sober and self-controlled and vigilant, and to resist the devil. But we can uncover the subtleties of Satan's schemes can be uncovered only through prayer and careful discernment—and we can resist him only by putting on the *full* armor of God.

The Full Armor of God: The Whole Church

All of the devil's schemes demand that we put on the *full* armor of God, not just one or two pieces. Overcoming the whole counsel of hell requires the whole counsel of God, which brings us to another crucial point. No one person has the whole counsel of God, especially in the broader aspects of spiritual warfare.

Rarely will spiritual warfare bring you face-to-face alone with the devil. Even overcoming personal temptations often requires the support of other caring and praying people. Spiritual warfare is an activity of the whole body of Christ working together. Jesus promised that the gates, or counsels, of hell would not prevail against the church.

Tragically, few Christians, especially in North America, where we pride ourselves on our individuality, understand our relationship to the whole. Every member of the body of Christ has a gift and a function. Any member detached from his place in the body is powerless, even lifeless. There are few things more ghastly than a dismembered human body. Perhaps the Lord Jesus feels the same about His body when its members fight among themselves and everyone does what is right in his own eyes.

The Greek of the New Testament, like many other languages, distinguishes between the singular and plural forms of *you,* both in the pronouns and in the endings of the verbs. Few English readers realize that nearly every *you* in the New Testament is actually plural. Using the phrase "you together" is probably a more accurate way to translate the plural Greek *you.* Look at Ephesians 6:13 in this light:

> Therefore *you together* put on the full armor of God [help each other get dressed for battle], so that when the day of evil comes, *you together* may be able to stand your ground, and after *you together* have done everything, to stand.

Spiritual warfare is body ministry. Each of us must stand up to the devil, but ultimately it's not something any of us can do on our own. When there is spiritual agreement, the power of God's people multiplies exponentially. "You *together* will pursue your enemies, and they will fall by the sword before you. Five of you will chase a hundred, and a hundred of you will chase ten thousand, and your enemies will fall by the sword before you" (Leviticus 26:7-8).

So resist the powers of darkness by putting on the full armor of God. Do it now. Do it together, beginning with the belt of truth.

THREE

The Belt of Truth

Stand firm then, with the belt of truth buckled around your waist.
EPHESIANS 6:14

O ur youngest son, Matthew, had just finished kindergarten. One of the members of our congregation made him a wooden chair, shaped and painted black and white like a Holstein cow. One day my wife discovered this little masterpiece of country folk art broken into two pieces.

I interrogated Matt to find out just how this had happened. "My friend Amy. She broke it," he replied confidently. "I was just standing there."

I persisted with the cross-examination: "Did you have *anything* to do with this at all?" Matt looked up at me with his best innocent face: "No, Dad, *really!*"

But something deep in my heart said to me, *This kid is not telling me the whole story.* So I warned him, "Next time Amy comes over to play, I'm going to ask her what really happened."

I knew full well that Matt would not like this proposal. Amy is a couple of years older and has more savvy—and a better memory, I suspected.

"If you are not telling me the whole story, Matt, if Amy tells me something different, you'll be in deep trouble. But I won't punish you if you tell me the truth now."

He studied me for a moment and, without saying another word, hopped away into another room. I was disappointed. My strategy had failed. Strange, isn't it, how a five-year-old can be so controlling!

But after about fifteen minutes, he came back into the front room and sat quietly on the sofa. I watched him over the top of my newspaper as he stared up at the wall. I knew what was going through his little mind, and I was supremely delighted. He was about to tell the truth!

I reopened the conversation: "Do you want to tell me what really happened now?"

"Yes," he answered. With surprising objectivity for a five-year-old, he recounted the incident. He had stood on the cow, he reported, grabbed it by the head, and given it a few brutal shakes. Amy had done the same thing, and the unfortunate wooden animal had collapsed on the bedroom floor.

"Matt!" I exclaimed. "I am so happy you told me the truth!" And I was. To me, telling the truth was far more important than whether or not he broke one of his toys. Kids will be kids. Kids will make mistakes, but truthfulness is forever. To put it in biblical terms, Matt was putting on the belt of truth.

What Is It?

"Stand firm then, with the belt of truth buckled around your waist." The belt of truth is the first of the six elements of armor in Ephesians 6. What is the belt of truth?

Perhaps we should begin by talking about what it is not. The belt of truth, in this context, is *not* merely correct creed or doctrinal orthodoxy. Nor is the belt of truth the same as the sword of the Spirit, "which is the Word of God," something Paul addresses a few verses later. As we will see, the sword of the Spirit is an *offensive* weapon, the power of God's Word. The belt of truth, on the other hand, refers to the condition of your private life, truth inside of you—truth guarding your private parts, so to speak. I like the mildly vulgar translation of the old King James Bible: "Gird up your loins with truth!"

The classic commentary *Expositor's Greek Testament* describes the belt of truth as "the personal grace of *candor, sincerity, truthfulness* ... [And] the mind that will practice no deceits and attempt no disguises is indeed vital to Christian safety."[1]

The aggressiveness of your public confession ("the sword of the Spirit") can never be a substitute for personal integrity ("the belt of truth") and an inner life that relates properly to God. People see your outward behaviors, but God sees into your heart. No doubt this is why the first step in preparing for spiritual battle is to put on the belt of truth. You must ensure that everything in your private life, as far as you know, is right with God.

You cannot even begin to think of standing up to the devil unless you are first committed to personal integrity. Public confessions of faith and public ministry are powerless if you are not "girding up your loins" with the belt of truth. On the other hand, the collapse of ministry and the destruction of your life and home begin when you allow the tempter entrance into your heart. And this happens, literally, when you compromise your conscience and settle for anything less than the whole truth and nothing but the truth in your life.

Like Ananias and Sapphira in Acts, you may be lying to yourself, to others, and even to God—and be completely unaware that Satan has filled your heart. The belt of truth is not the facts you believe about the Bible. It's the way you live your life.

Telling Yourself the Truth

The ancient introduction to Psalm 51 tells us why King David wrote this psalm: "For the director of music. A psalm of David. When the prophet Nathan came to him after David had committed adultery with Bathsheba." Psalm 51 is about the devastating effects of private sin.

What happened? Standing on the roof of his palace, David saw beautiful Bathsheba bathing next door. It didn't seem to matter to him that he had his eyes on another man's wife. David's raging river of lust was so powerful that the consequences of sin seemed, for the moment, inconsequential. Besides, David was king. He could do anything he wanted. So he had Bathsheba brought to his palace, where he lay with her.

But Bathsheba became pregnant. Now David felt anxious, not because he had sinned but because he might get caught. Instead of confessing his evil to God and cleaning up his life, he schemed to exonerate himself. He manipulated people and circumstances so that he would not have to face himself and deal with his sin.

Bathsheba's husband, Uriah, was on active military duty. So David recalled him from the front lines of battle for some "R and R." David expected Uriah to have an evening or two with his wife. Her pregnancy, then, could be easily explained.

Uriah came home, but he slept on the front step of David's palace and refused to spend any time alone with his wife. How could he enjoy himself, he reasoned, when his comrades were sacrificing themselves on the field of battle?

Frustrated, David devised a dastardly plan. He prepared written orders to send Uriah into the battle and to abandon him in the thick of the fight, ensuring his death. And worse, he had Uriah deliver the sealed document—his own death certificate! What a great way to solve his problem, David presumed. Now he could marry this woman, and no one would discover his sin.

But the prophet Nathan exposed his king's treachery. He told David a heartrending story about a little pet lamb, confiscated from a poor family by an evil rich man. At first David wanted to throw the man into prison. But when he realized that he himself was the culprit in the parable, David's anger over the purported injustice turned to wrenching sorrow and repentance.

"Have mercy on me, O God, according to your unfailing love," David wept in anguish. "According to your great compassion blot out my transgressions. Wash away all my iniquity and cleanse me from my sin.... Against you, you only, have I sinned" (verses 1-4). And in verse 6 David conceded, "Surely you desire truth *in the inner parts*."

God does not have His eye on just my public behavior. He wants to shine the light of His Word into every crevice and corner of my mind. If He doesn't, I will not be prepared to resist and overcome my spiritual enemies.

Facing Denial

What is the belt of truth? Having a pure heart before God, or to say it another way, being honest with myself. The opposite of self-honesty is self-deception, something psychologists call denial.

Denial, for example, is a root of alcoholism. Alcohol is a substitute for facing oneself. It puts the mind to sleep. A heavy drinker can avoid thinking about his problems and facing reality. Most importantly, he avoids facing himself.

For someone who has a drinking problem, alcohol is not the real problem. The person is the problem, and the solution to the problem is being willing to face oneself. Denial is avoidance of that problem.

But denial is not just something people talk about in Alcoholics Anonymous. Every one of us has problems with denial. King David's initial denial was utterly irrational, but how often do we react the same way? "Who broke the toy, Matt?" "Amy broke it." Our lying, our deception, our manipulation of others, can be so clever we surprise ourselves!

Think about where you work. It may even be in a church! Are people around you always truthful? Are they honest with others? Are they honest with themselves? Are you honest with them?

We live in a society where lying and denial, double-talk and misinformation, are commonplace. A recent article on the front page of the *The Arizona Republic*, the principal newspaper in Phoenix, reported that Americans are increasingly unwilling to take responsibility for their behavior and, of course, are increasingly willing to blame others. In an American presidential election, the most important decision of our democratic process, few of us really know what to believe or who is telling the truth.

The problem of denial and self-deception is basic to virtually all of life's problems. Have you, for example, had your spouse or a friend become unexpectedly testy about something? And when you pressed the person, have you been told that he or she did not want to discuss it? Or worse, were you given some half-truth or maybe even made to feel guilty for asking?

What we are facing here is not merely a human problem. Satan is the great liar, and hell itself is the fountainhead of all deceit. In *People of the Lie*, psychiatrist and bestselling author M.Scott Peck writes:

As well as being the Father of Lies, Satan may be said to be a spirit of mental illness. In *The Road Less Traveled* I defined mental

health as "an ongoing process of dedication to reality at all costs."
Satan is utterly dedicated to opposing that process. In fact, the
best definition I have for Satan is that it is *a real spirit of unreal-
ity.* The paradoxical reality of this spirit must be recognized.[2]

Why do we lie? Why do we so easily deceive ourselves? We do it to
protect ourselves, we think, and yet the very thing we do to save our
skins is what destroys us. "The man who loves his life will lose it, while
the man who hates his life in this world will keep it" (John 12:25).

To have a pure heart before God means to be honest with oneself.
To put on the belt of truth means to first renounce the cover-up of
denial. Denial is false armor. Ironically, self-honesty feels like taking
something off, like undressing yourself! Yet it actually brings God into
your life, and you cannot ask for better protection than that!

An Age-Old Problem

The story of David is only one of many in the Bible about people who
would not face their sins, who would not face themselves. When
Adam and Eve sinned, God could not find them. "Why are you hiding?" He asked. "And those fig leaves? Why are you trying to protect
yourselves? Who told you that you were naked?"

Genesis 3:8-13 gives us the first recorded human conversation with
God after the Fall. Adam spoke first: "The woman [denial] whom *You*
gave me [more denial], she made me eat." Then Eve: "The devil made
me do it [still more denial]."

Genesis 4 tells the story of Cain and Abel. Cain's offering of grain
was not acceptable to God, which made him very angry about the
apparent injustice of God's favor toward his brother, Abel. Surprisingly,

God never really told him *why* his offering was unacceptable, but He warned Cain that his response was crucial. Sin was lurking at his door, waiting to consume him.

We cannot always guarantee God's response to our "offerings," but regardless of what happens, regardless of what we *think* should happen, we are always responsible for our reactions. I am never accountable for what God does or does not do. I am always accountable for me.

Cain refused to take responsibility for his attitudes and behavior, went out into the field, and killed his brother.

"Where is Abel?" God inquired of Cain.

"I don't know. Am I my brother's keeper?" Cain was unwilling to be honest with himself.

And then there was Aaron's peculiar behavior at Sinai, told in Exodus 32. God was giving the Law to Moses, and it was taking an interminably long time. The Israelites did not even know if Moses was still alive, and no one dared ascend the mountain to look for him, what with all of that lightning and thunder. So they insisted on creating their own god. Aaron buckled under their demand and fashioned a golden calf.

As Moses returned from the mountain, he was puzzled by all the commotion in the camp. When he saw the Israelites worshiping the golden image, he smashed the tablets of stone, symbolizing the broken covenant. In anger and disbelief he demanded an explanation.

Aaron's response was audacious denial: "Do not be angry, my lord. You know how prone *these people* are to evil." Unbelievable! Aaron was the ringleader! And then this: "So I told them, 'Whoever has any gold jewelry, take it off.' Then they gave me the gold, and I threw it into the fire, *and out came this calf!*" (verse 24).

We laugh at Aaron's ridiculous excuse. It reminds us of something a kid will say when caught with a hand in the cookie jar. But it's really not funny. Denial is the terrible root of all human sin: Adam and Eve disobeying God. Cain killing his brother. Aaron and the Israelites worshiping an idol. David committing adultery and murder. It is no different today.

The Consequences of Denial

At least three things happen when we indulge in persistent denial. *First,* denial alienates us from God. We cannot stand before His righteousness. Look at Adam and Eve hiding in the Garden.

Second, denial alienates us from one another. Cain's murderous anger is an example. I just read in the newspaper that a man in a rage ran over three people with his truck, all because of an argument over who would bring home the beer. Denial destroys relationships. Sometimes it even destroys other people, because the one who denies his own sin must blame someone else. "Scapegoating" is what we call it. "The woman, she made me eat the forbidden fruit," said Adam.

Third, denial causes us to self-destruct. David confessed, "When I remained silent and refused to confess my sins, when I would not face myself, my bones wasted away and my strength was sapped as in the heat of summer" (Psalm 32:3-4, my paraphrase). God forgave him, but David's kingdom was never the same after his little fling with adultery.

God is incredibly patient. Sometimes He allows scandal to go on for years in nationally known Christian ministries. Then somebody finds out, and the news hits the media fan. Sooner or later, sin has a payback.

For someone who is in denial, life will *always* get worse before it gets better, unless there is repentance and change. The apostle Paul wrote, "If we judged ourselves, we would not come under judgment" (1 Corinthians 11:31). But judging ourselves—healthy self-examination—is impossible when you are bound by denial.

Denial and Spiritual Warfare

It was the evening before I first preached a message on the belt of truth. I was out jogging, thinking hard about my sermon and its implications. Suddenly the whole issue of spiritual deception hit me like a bolt of lightning.

Do you know why self-deception, denial, and lying are so terrible? Because those are the tactics of Satan himself, who is the Father of Lies, *and he attaches himself to dishonest people.* Denial is spiritually dangerous.

The end result, then, of the unhappy consequences of dishonesty is that *it may open you up to the direct oppression and control of the devil.* This is certainly the logic of Ephesians 6. If our battle is not with flesh and blood, if we have an adversary who is trying to destroy us, we must shield ourselves with the armor of God. Taking up the belt of truth, the first step, keeps us out of the steel trap of self-deception, out of the clutches of Satan.

Scott Peck argues in *People of the Lie* that persistent denial may actually allow the entrance into our lives of evil spirits, which cement our sin in virtually unbreakable behavioral problems. Charlene is a case study to which he devotes a lengthy chapter. Later in the book he concludes:

When I was working with her I felt almost overwhelmed by Charlene's sickness. I wasn't sure I had the power to cure her. Now, in fact, I know that I, alone, did not and still do not have the power and that the psychoanalytic method I used was not wholly the right approach to her. Then I knew no other way to go. Today is different. I do know another approach, far more appropriate and possibly effective in such a case. Today, if I could see evidence that a healthy part of her wanted the whole to be healed, I would with conviction and authority offer Charlene the possible means of her salvation: deliverance and exorcism.[3]

This is spiritual warfare!

Listen to what Paul writes to the Thessalonians: "The coming of the lawless one [the Antichrist] will be in accordance with the work of Satan displayed ... in every sort of evil that deceives those who are perishing. They perish *because they refused to love the truth* and so be saved. For this reason God sends them *a powerful delusion* so that they will believe the lie" (2 Thessalonians 2:9-11).

What people believe or refuse to believe about God and about themselves is influenced by the Father of Lies himself. Peter rebuked Ananias, "How is it that Satan has so filled your heart that you have lied to the Holy Spirit?" (Acts 5:3).

The Power of Personal Confession

You can practice personal honesty by making yourself accountable to another person you trust. You need someone to whom you can speak openly about your fears, failures, and sins. Kurt Koch, author of numerous books on the occult and demonization, writes in *Christian Counseling and Occultism:*

> The taking of refuge in secrecy is a characteristic feature of the powers of darkness. The demonic tempter always lives by the power of the secrecy which exists between him and us. As long as there are certain things kept secret in our life, which no man may know, the crafty enemy will have dominion over our soul. As soon, however, as the secret is told and betrayed, the power of darkness loses its claim of dominion over us. Hence, confession is a counter-action against the kingdom of darkness.[4]

I was speaking at a Youth With A Mission discipleship school in Oregon, and a young man asked if we could spend some time together. He was still reeling from the recent breakup of his church, where he had served faithfully as an associate pastor for several years. He could not free himself from obsessive thoughts about his perceived failure in his relationship with his former pastor.

After talking for nearly two hours, I asked him if he would like to pray. He said yes. I asked him to echo my words as I led him in a confession of release. Suddenly, at the crucial point in the prayer of release, he became utterly mute. He was unable to repeat what I had just spoken.

It was a moment of crisis and change. He was about to be liberated from spiritual oppression. He stared at me with teary eyes and confessed, "Man, is this hard!"

Taking a deep breath and fighting for his emotional life, he continued his prayer, and God powerfully released him. He was free. His personal confession to me, coupled with the two of us agreeing in prayer, were the keys to his deliverance. I doubt that he could have had a similar experience on his own.

"Confess your sins to each other," James wrote, "and pray for each other so that you may be healed. The prayer of a righteous man is powerful and effective" (James 5:16).

Resisting the Father of Lies

Resistance to the Father of Lies begins with an uncompromising, unwavering commitment to the truth and truthfulness, especially with yourself. Listen to Paul's resolve:

> We have renounced disgraceful ways—secret thoughts, feelings, desires and underhandedness, methods and arts that men hide through shame; we refuse to deal craftily (to practice trickery and cunning) or to adulterate or handle dishonestly the Word of God; but we state the truth openly—clearly and candidly.
>
> 2 CORINTHIANS 4:2, AMPLIFIED

Recognize that you have an adversary who specializes in lies and half-truths, and refuse to identify yourself with him and his schemes. Instead, repent. Turn away from the fig leaves of self-protection and put on the covering of God, the belt of truth. Put on the armor of God as if your life depended on it, for it does.

A Prayer for Putting on the Belt of Truth

Dear Lord Jesus, You are the Way, *the Truth*, and the Life. I turn away from dishonesty and distortion. I put on the belt of truth. I renounce the devil, who is the Father of Lies.

Help me to be honest with myself and with others. Let me be like Your disciple Nathaniel, of whom You said, "Behold, a man in whom there is no guile." Deliver me from defensiveness and the blindness that does not let me see myself as You see me and as others see me.

I recognize that the only way I will ever change is to see where I need to change. I must be honest with myself, even if it hurts, because it will hurt even more if I do not change.

Forgive me for blaming others, for holding others responsible for my problems. I take responsibility for my feelings and behaviors.

In Jesus' mighty name, Amen.

FOUR

The Breastplate of Righteousness

Stand firm then with the breastplate of righteousness in place.
EPHESIANS 6:14

It was the late 1960s. Our college soccer team made a road trip to
Stanford University. There, on the public mall of a great American
university, I was eyewitness to some bizarre rites we had been seeing on
television. Right in front of me was a large group of Hare Krishnas
doing their sacred dance and offering onlookers their holy food: pop-
corn.

I refused their offer and continued staring. Except for their shaven
heads and saffron robes, they looked like any other young Americans.

Some of our guys began sharing Christ with them, but they
responded with religious scorn. I remember one of them ridiculing my
friend's athletic bag: "Why do you fool with such nonsense?" The
implication, of course, was that if we were really interested in religion,
we would abstain from everything worldly, including sports.

Unfortunately, there are many Christians who feel the same way.
Righteousness, for them, is a list of do's and don'ts. The more carefully
you define your list, the more righteous you will be.

Overuse, abuse, and misconceptions have made the term *righteousness* virtually meaningless. More often than not it has a negative
connotation. Even if we understand it correctly, righteousness is something we humans are likely to shun: "The sinful mind is hostile to

God. It does not submit to God's law, nor can it do so" (Romans 8:7).

So in order to understand the breastplate of righteousness, we must explore the biblical concept of righteousness and its relationship to spiritual warfare. We must also learn how to overcome the temptation to sin.

What Is Righteousness?

Paul probably had Isaiah 59 in mind when he wrote about the armor of God:

> The Lord looked and was displeased that there was no justice. He was appalled that there was no one to intercede; so his own arm worked salvation for him, and his own righteousness sustained him. *He put on righteousness as his breastplate,* and the helmet of salvation on his head.
>
> ISAIAH 59:15-17

The "breastplate of righteousness" originates with God Himself, which means that righteousness can be understood only in its relation to the divine nature. In fact, the whole armor of God is a revelation of the whole character of God. To study the armor of God is to study God's attributes. To put on the armor is to put on God's qualities: truth, righteousness, peace, faith, and salvation.

Conversely, a study of the armor of God also opens up possibilities for a better understanding of the nature of the enemy we are fighting. Satan is a kind of spiritual antimatter. Whatever God is, Satan isn't.

God is light; Satan is darkness. God is truth and truthful; Satan is the Father of Lies, the great deceiver, and the master of distortion. Jesus is the Prince of Peace; Satan is the underlying cause of strife and chaos. Jesus is the Author and Finisher of our faith; Satan is the proponent of unbelief. God gives salvation and life; Satan seeks to steal, kill, and destroy.

With regard to righteousness, Satan's plan is to repress it and foster instead either sin or false righteousness—human effort to meet the standards of God. Righteousness that's not grounded in the nature of God and imparted to us by God's grace is a righteousness of rules. Legalism is righteousness without relationship, regulations without love. In contrast, true righteousness flows out of our personal friendship with the Father.

Righteousness Out of Relationship

Imagine that one day your doorbell rings, and there standing on your porch are three children. They offer you a shocking proposal. After shopping around the neighborhood, they have decided to ask you to become their parent, but they would like to know the rules of your household before making a final commitment. They have been searching, they tell you, for the ideal family, and they are willing to *prove* they are worthy of your love by obeying your rules. And as long as they obey the rules, they expect you to love and care for them.

Strange scenario? Not really! This is the way many Christians think about their relationship with God. They would agree that He is their Father, but only conditionally. If they do what is right, they reason, God will keep loving them. If they don't, well, maybe He will, maybe He won't.

This is not the Bible's idea of righteousness by grace through faith. We Christians are not God's children because we have impressed Him with our good works and carefully obeyed all His family rules. We are His children by birth, by being born of the Spirit. This new birth brings a dramatic change in our nature and in our relationship with God.

To the unbeliever, God is a judge. A judge, of course, bases his decisions on the way the accused obeys—or disobeys—the rules. For a judge, relationship is not relevant. In fact, if you go to court for some reason and you discover, to your surprise, that the judge is a relative, well, that judge will be reassigned!

Now, the Christian, someone who has become a member of the family of God by believing in Jesus, has God as his or her Father. And for a father, relationship is the bottom line, not rules. Jesus illustrated this in the parable of the Prodigal Son. The father, in overwhelming love for his wayward son, forgives and forgets his child's sinful choices.

True righteousness, then, is grounded in a relationship of grace. God, the fearsome Judge, becomes our loving Father. When Jesus comes into our hearts by faith, we are born again. Paul the apostle describes our transformation this way:

> Since we have now been justified by his [Jesus'] blood, how much more shall we be saved from God's wrath through him! For if, when we were God's enemies, we were reconciled to him through the death of his Son, how much more, having been reconciled, shall we be saved through his life!
>
> ROMANS 5:9-10

Righteousness, therefore, is not just what we do; it's who we are. Before being saved, a person is a sinner by nature, not merely because he or she commits sin. This is why Jesus said we must be born again. In other words, we need a new nature. Jesus died not only for our *sins,* plural; when He was crucified, our *sin nature* was nailed to the cross with Him. The cross of Christ offers us a kind of legal exchange: Jesus takes my sin in exchange for his perfect righteousness. "God made [Jesus] who had no sin to be sin for us," Paul tells us, "so that in him we might become the righteousness of God" (2 Corinthians 5:21).

Righteousness grounded in the nature of God, therefore, is *imputed* to (a theological term meaning "given to and placed in") those who trust in Jesus Christ. Paul used Abraham's experience with God to illustrate this doctrine: "Abraham believed God, and it was credited to him as righteousness" (Romans 4:3). When we first believe in Christ, the debt of our unrighteousness is paid and the very righteousness of God is credited to our spiritually bankrupt account.

Our relationship with God, then, is not based on what we have done but on the legal transfer of Christ's righteousness to us. When the Father sees us born again, impregnated with a new nature, clothed with the robe of the righteousness of Christ Himself, He receives us to Himself as one of His very own—and loves us unconditionally. In the words of the great hymn:

> *My hope is built on nothing less*
> *than Jesus' blood and righteousness.*

Righteousness and God's Laws

What value, then, do the laws of God have for the believer? Everything. God's laws are not a means of eternal salvation but are certainly a revelation of the One who is the Author of the Law. Obedience to God's Word—that is, the practice of righteousness—lines us up with God's order.

Doing good works will never get you to heaven; only God's grace in Christ can do that. But obeying the Word will release the blessing of God into your earthly life, keep you away from the things that will damage your life, and make you eligible for heavenly rewards.

God's law, or God's Word, is God's authority, and obedience places you under the protective covering of His authority. Just like the Prodigal Son, disobedience does not take you out of relationship with the Father, but it certainly takes you out of His home and lands you in the muddy pigpen of your own sin. Defined simply, *righteousness is doing what is right.* "Dear children," John wrote, "do not let anyone lead you astray. *He who does what is right is righteous"* (1 John 3:7).

God's law, His Word, brings order into our troubled lives. The root of the Greek term *dike,* which is translated "righteousness" or "justice," means literally "to give direction, to establish." Righteousness gives your life direction and establishes it on the rock of God's character. In other words, *doing what is right is good for you!* You are the beneficiary of right living.

The Scriptures are commonly called *The Holy Bible.* Perhaps a better title would be *Father Knows Best.* God's Word does not restrict us; it saves our lives. The Bible is like a manufacturer's instruction manual. Who would think of operating an expensive piece of high-tech medical equipment without a manual—and an expert to help you understand the manual? And yet so many people pay no attention to the life guidelines written by the Creator of life Himself.

My wife and I raised three children, and each one had to be taught to be careful when crossing the street. I even had to punish them occasionally for ignoring my stern warnings about the dangers of oncoming traffic. From their small-minded, preschool point of view, I was trying to limit their freedom. But no, I had their very best interests in mind. I loved them too much to let them kill themselves!

God's Word is like that. It's our loving Father telling us how we can keep from killing ourselves!

Living Together?

One of the most difficult things I face as a pastor, for example, is challenging young couples to maintain their sexual purity before marriage. At any given time, our church has dozens of couples in our pre-marriage counseling program. Surprisingly, a large proportion of the couples who want to enter the program are already living together. Many are new Christians with unformed convictions, but many should know better. The world's way of doing things can have a powerful influence on the best of us.

In conjunction with our pre-marriage counseling, we ask couples not to live with one another. Our rationale is God's Word. We assume that if the Bible is against premarital sex, then abstinence is not only right, it's good for the couple's long-term relationship. And, oh, do some people object! Some even opt to be married somewhere else, even though it is commonly known that people who live together before marriage are more likely to divorce than those who don't.

I have often asked couples, "What if we were living in a country where being a Christian was against the law? Suppose you received Christ and were baptized, and word reached your employer. You knew that within a week you would lose your job. If you asked me for counsel, what would you expect me to tell you as your pastor? What if I suggested, 'Don't worry. Deny Christ. You need your job to support your family. God will forgive you'? Would you trust me as your spiritual leader?"

Doing what is right is no easy road, but there are few better shields for repelling the fiery darts of the enemy and helping you stand strong. Like the small end of a funnel, the narrow gate, the right way, offers few options, and sometimes only one, but ultimately it leads to the broad spectrum of God's blessing and life. The wide gate is like the same funnel in reverse. It has multiple options, all of which lead to only one consequence—death (see Matthew 7:13-14). "There is a way that seems right to us, but the end of that way is death" (Proverbs 16:25).

Disobedience and Spiritual Conflict

If doing what is right is good for you, then failing to do the right thing—disobedience—is self-destructive and may even invite Satan's intrusion into your life. As the apostle Paul wrote, "As for you, you were dead in your transgressions and sins, in which you used to live when you followed the ways of this world and of the ruler of the king-dom of the air, *the spirit who is now at work in those who are disobedi-ent*"(Ephesians 2:1-2).

Jesus taught His disciples the peril of unrighteousness. Shortly before His crucifixion He announced to them, "The prince of this world is coming. He has no hold on me" (John 14:30). Satan tempted Jesus, the Last Adam, hoping for a replay of man's fall in the Garden of Eden. But Jesus resisted the temptation to sin and refused to give the devil a place in His life. The breastplate of righteousness is an essential defense in spiritual warfare.

Paul picks up on this idea of giving the devil a place in your life. "In your anger," he wrote, "do not sin. Do not let the sun go down while you are still angry, *and do not give the devil a foothold*" (Ephesians 4:26-27). If we let our anger go unchecked, if we are persistently unrighteous, we risk exposing ourselves to direct demonic influence.

Merrill Unger, the renowned Old Testament scholar, wrote in *Demons in the World Today*, "It is possible for a believer to experience severe demon influence or obsession if he persistently yields to demonic temptation and sin."[1] We *must* crucify our carnal natures and overcome temptation.

Understanding and Overcoming Temptation

Living righteously requires an understanding of the nature of temptation and how to overcome it. A master key in spiritual warfare is recognizing the part you play, because temptation really starts with you! Binding the devil is directly related to restraining yourself.

As we saw earlier, the apostle Peter commands us to be sober and vigilant, "self-controlled and alert" (1 Peter 5:8). Why? Because our adversary the devil is prowling around like a roaring lion, looking for someone to devour. Jesus once told Peter, "Satan hath desired to have you" (Luke 22:31, KJV).

So what goes through your mind when you are tempted? What do you do about it? How do you handle yourself?

The truth of the matter is that you are not influenced just by the temptation itself. Temptation is not what happens to you; it's what happens in you. The moment something comes into your life to test you, to tempt you, the inner you becomes a tangle of warring thoughts and potentially wrong responses. You may be tempted sexually or by materialism, but those kinds of things only bring out the real you.

Like Adam and Eve, our real problem is not with the forbidden fruit but with ourselves. And this is precisely what James teaches us in the first chapter of his little epistle:

One: Take Personal Responsibility (Verse 12)

Blessed is the man who perseveres under trial, because when he has stood the test, he will receive the crown of life that God has promised to those who love him.

In order to overcome temptation and resist the devil, we must take responsibility for our attitudes and behaviors. We cannot control what happens to us, but by God's grace we can control our responses.

A friend and I were discussing the untimely death of a Christian woman. She was young and full of faith—disturbingly full of faith, because anyone with as much faith as she seemed to have just shouldn't die.

I will never forget what my friend mumbled to me in the quiet of the church foyer the day of her funeral, *"Victorious Christian living is not coming to some place in life where you don't have any more problems."*

No, victory in Christ means that we can be more than conquerors right in the middle of the problem. Whether or not the problem or temptation goes away, we must cling tenaciously to Jesus.

I cannot always control circumstances or their ultimate outcome. I cannot always choose what happens to me. But I can choose my attitudes and behaviors in the face of what happens. I will be tempted. That's inevitable. But I don't have to give in to the temptation.

Two: Don't Blame Others (Verse 13)

When tempted, no one should say, "God is tempting me." For God cannot be tempted by evil, nor does he tempt anyone.

Jesus could not control the people who crucified Him, although He could have called a legion of angels to His defense. He chose instead to control His response: "Father, forgive them, for they do not know what they are doing" (Luke 23:34). When He was reviled, He did not revile back but committed everything to the Father (see 1 Peter 2:23).

Jesus took personal responsibility for His feelings, for His response to a situation in His life that simply was not going to change, and He refused to blame anyone else for what was happening to Him. He didn't even blame His heavenly Father, although He knew it was the Father's will for Him to die.

I will say it again: It is impossible to take personal responsibility for your feelings and behaviors if you persist in blaming others for the troubles of your life. This is the heart of what James is saying in 1:13: "When tempted, no one should say, 'God is tempting me.' For God cannot be tempted by evil, nor does He tempt anyone." God is certainly not the one who tempts us.

We can't even blame the devil for our problems, even though he is the eternal tempter. The-devil-made-me-do-it philosophy of life is *not* biblical. In fact, this is one of Satan's schemes. If he can get you to blame him for your inability to resist temptation, then he has gained a great victory. He is more than willing to take the blame if it means you will not change. If you don't take responsibility for your response to the temptation, you will never overcome it. Be self-controlled and alert, for your adversary the devil, like a roaring lion, is on the hunt.

In the classic little book *Why Am I Afraid to Tell You Who I Am?*, best-selling author John Powell tells the story of the syndicated columnist Sydney Harris, who once accompanied a friend of his to the newsstand.

Accepting the newspaper which was shoved rudely in his direction, the friend of Harris politely smiled and wished the newsman a nice weekend. As the two friends walked down the street, the columnist asked:

"Does he always treat you so rudely?"

"Yes, unfortunately, he does."

"And are you always so polite and friendly to him?"

"Yes, I am."

"Why are you so nice to him when he is so unfriendly to you?"

"Because I don't want *him* to decide how I'm going to act," his friend replied. "I'm not going to allow the way he acts to determine how I feel inside or how I respond."[2]

We cannot always control what happens to us. We will be tempted to sin, but we must take personal responsibility for our response to every temptation. Don't blame God; He tempts no one. Don't blame the devil; he doesn't *make* you do anything. And don't blame others.

Don't even blame yourself. Paul wrote to the Corinthians, "I care very little if I am judged by you or by any human court; indeed, I do not even judge myself. My conscience is clear" (1 Corinthians 4:3-4).

There is a great difference between blaming yourself and taking responsibility. It is one thing to say, "I'm going to make the best of this situation." It's quite another to say, "Poor me. I'm such a terrible person. My failure brought this on."

Self-pity is nothing more than emotional penance. Beating yourself up with "poor me's" will not heal your soul. In fact, that can actually be just another subtle way to avoid taking personal responsibility for your feelings and behavior.

No one makes me feel the way I do. Not the guy at the newsstand, not my wife, not my children, not my neighbor, not my boss—not even the devil! *I* make me feel the way I do. And it is impossible for me to overcome temptation if I am blind to myself.

Three: Understand Yourself and the Nature of Temptation (Verses 14-15)

But each one is tempted when, by his own evil desire, he is dragged away and enticed. Then, after desire has conceived, it gives birth to sin; and sin, when it is full-grown, gives birth to death.

Temptation begins with an unwillingness to take personal responsibility for our feelings and behaviors. Temptation without human weakness is like a seed without water. Bait is not the reason fish bite; they bite because they are hungry. "Each one is tempted when, by his own evil desire, he is dragged away and enticed" (James 1:14). My battle is not with temptation but with myself.

The Greek term used here, *epithumia*—translated "evil desire" or "lust"—can be used in either a positive or negative sense. It means, more accurately, "great desire." Jesus used the term at the Last Supper: "I have *eagerly desired* to eat this Passover with you before I suffer" (Luke 22:15). Paul also used the term in a powerfully positive sense when he wrote, "I *desire* to depart and be with Christ, which is better by far" (Philippians 1:23).

In other words, we cannot assume that James' use of *epithumia* is necessarily negative. In fact, the context seems to bear this out. According to James, *epithumia*—strong desire or passion—is not sin unless that strong desire "has conceived" (1:15). My point is that a strong desire is not in itself sin. Our human passions are the targets of temptation, but sin occurs only when we succumb to the temptation and surrender our will to the passions of the flesh.

Christians may never call their feelings "sinful," but what we say about our feelings suggests otherwise. I do not know how many people have apologized to me for crying during a counseling session. I often have to tell people that it's OK to cry. I have to remind them that Jesus felt deep emotion, too.

The shortest verse in the Bible is one of the most touching: "Jesus wept." We have a High Priest who feels what we feel, who hurts when we hurt, and who holds us in His arms when we cry. "Blessed are those who mourn, for they shall be comforted."

My passions and desires, like my God-given sexuality, are not evil unless I use them for sinful purposes. Passion in and of itself is not sinful; it's just human. Jesus, a man of deep passions and one who was tempted just as you and I are, died not to deliver us from our human passions but to deliver our human passions from the power of sin.

When our passions give in to sin, though, it opens up all kinds of possibilities for evil. Sin, James wrote, when it has become "full grown," results in death. It is one thing to fall into sin, to give in to your passions from time to time. It is quite another to give yourself over to the lusts of the flesh, to let sin become a behavior pattern.

An occasional trespass is relatively easy to overcome, but habits of sin are very difficult to break, and they invariably lead to death. James is using the term *death*, I believe, in its inclusive sense—death in all its forms: spiritual and physical, emotional and relational. "There is a way that seems right to a man, but in the end it leads to death" (Proverbs 14:12).

Listen to what Paul wrote to Timothy in this regard:

> Those who oppose him [the Lord's servant] he must gently instruct, in the hope that God will grant them repentance leading them to a knowledge of the truth, and that they will come to their senses and escape from the trap of the devil, who has taken them captive to do his will.
>
> 2 TIMOTHY 2:25

When people reject the truth and give in to temptation, they "undress" themselves. Without the breastplate of righteousness, they stand naked before the devil. Without a firm commitment to resist temptation, they risk becoming spiritual captives, bound to patterns of sin and bound to the devil to do his will.

May I remind you again that we have a High Priest, the Lord Jesus, who understands our temptations and knows our weaknesses. He was tempted just as we are, and "because he himself suffered when he was tempted, he is able to help those who are being tempted" (Hebrews 2:18).

Jesus understands what you are facing.

Jesus feels what you are feeling.

Jesus wants to help you endure temptation and overcome it.

The night is nearly over; the day is almost here. So let us put aside the deeds of darkness and put on the armor of light. Clothe yourselves with the Lord Jesus Christ, and do not think about how to gratify the desires of the sinful nature.

ROMANS 13:12-14

A Prayer for Putting on the Breastplate of Righteousness

Heavenly Father, righteous God, I thank You that my relationship with You is based on the righteousness of Your Son Jesus. I stand in Your grace. I could never be good enough in myself to come to You or to stand against the devil.

Thank You, Lord, for the righteousness of Christ deposited into my heavenly bank account. I make a withdrawal to take care of my needs today. I stand shielded by the breastplate of Your perfect and permanent righteousness. I am also determined to honor Your laws, to obey Your Word, and to do what is right.

In the name of Jesus, I resist the temptation to sin, to enter the wide gate, to walk down the path of least resistance, to do what is wrong. In the name of Jesus, I resist the devil, the one who has been breaking Your laws from the beginning.

You, God, are my righteousness, and I will live in obedience to Your Word. You are my Father, and You know best. In Jesus' mighty name, Amen.

FIVE

The Readiness of Peace

Stand firm then with your feet fitted with the readiness that comes from the gospel of peace.

EPHESIANS 6:14-15

As a pastor, I find that the greatest challenge of full-time ministry is people! Our church staff has often joked, "If we didn't have so many people around here, we wouldn't have all these problems."

I have tried to ward off church strife by pasting Romans 14:19 on my office door: "Let us therefore *make every effort* to do what leads to peace and to mutual edification." I don't want anyone entering my office without first coming under the authority of that Scripture. I wish I could say it works!

People, even pastors and church leaders, are generally unaware of the dramatic impact their attitudes and words can have on others. The writer of Hebrews warns us, "See to it that no bitter root grows up to cause trouble and defile many" (Hebrews 12:15).

But here is the stinger: People are even less aware that their not-so-godly attitudes—and their "sincere and honest" comments that hide those attitudes—may actually be influenced by demons. The Bible presents this as a possibility. The "wisdom" of "bitter envy and selfish ambition," James writes, "does not come down from heaven but is earthly, unspiritual, *of the devil* [and] there you find disorder and every evil practice" (James 3:14-16). Maybe this is why James also writes earlier in his letter, "Everyone should be quick to listen, slow to speak and slow to become angry" (James 1:19).

Sometimes even well-meaning words, ill-timed and thoughtlessly spoken, can have the bite of a scorpion. When Jesus predicted His death, Peter reacted with all the best intentions: "You'll never die, Lord. I won't let that happen, even if I have to give up my own life for You."

Jesus recognized instantly the demonic source of Peter's impetuous remark: "Out of my sight, Satan! You are a stumbling block to me; you do not have in mind the things of God, but the things of men" (Matthew 16:23).

Not every divisive attitude or comment is devilish, but many are. This is why Paul expects every believer to have his feet "fitted with the readiness that comes from the gospel of peace," so that we will be able to stand up and fight "when the day of evil comes." We have to learn how to make peace, not war.

Now, this may seem to contradict the very message of this book: spiritual warfare. But listen again carefully to one of our key verses in this book: "Our warfare is *not* with flesh and blood." In other words, God's command to believers is to stand and fight the devil, not one another. We actually resist the devil and his schemes when we keep the unity of the Spirit in the bond of peace.

While Satan is aggressively making war, we must be aggressively making peace. Peace is part of the full armor of God. There are three important terms in Ephesians 6:15 that bear our attention: *the gospel of peace, readiness,* and *feet.*

The Gospel of Peace

The gospel of peace is, simply, the good news of peace. The Greek word translated *gospel* means "good message." *Evangelist*, which means "messenger of good," is an English word derived from this same Greek term. Specifically, the gospel is the good news of peace with God through Jesus Christ. "Glory to God in the highest, and *on earth peace*" was the heavenly anthem heralding the first Christmas (Luke 2:14).

The biblical idea of peace is comprehensive. It includes peace of mind, but there is much more. Peace in the Bible has to do ultimately with our relationship with God. Personal wholeness begins only when we are reconciled to God.

Sin is a declaration of war. The death of Christ on the cross was God's offer of peace. Jesus actually took the blame for our sin, and when we come to Him in faith, our wrong standing with God is made right. "Since we have been justified through faith, we have peace with God through our Lord Jesus Christ" (Romans 5:1).

Thus, the healing of our broken relationship with the Father is the most important kind of peace. It is the restoration of *shalom,* the common but comprehensive Hebrew term translated "peace." The *Theological Wordbook of the Old Testament* tells us that the "general meaning behind the root *sh-l-m* is of completion and fulfillment—of entering into a state of wholeness and unity, a restored relationship. [It means] peace, prosperity, health, completeness, safety."[1]

Shalom is everything that's right. It could even be said that the word *shalom* in the Old Testament took on messianic overtones. The Hebrews believed they would never realize true peace, security, wholeness, and even national restoration until the coming of the Messiah to establish God's kingdom in the earth. Satan has made war on the saints, but God's kingdom will prevail. Isaiah prophesied:

For to us a child is born and the government will be on his
shoulders. And he will be called Prince of Peace [*shalom*]. Of the
increase of his government and peace [*shalom*] there will be no
end. He will reign on David's throne upholding it with justice
and righteousness from that time on and forever.

ISAIAH 9:6-7

Shalom is everything right with God. *Shalom* is also everything right
in my relationships with family and friends. "Implicit in *shalom* is the
idea of unimpaired relationships with others."[2]

Here is where we cross the line and the real battles of daily life
begin—in relationships. Satan will do everything in his power to keep
us out of relationship with God. Once we are justified and have peace
with God, the devil will do everything in his power to keep us out of
relationship with one another. It took a mighty act of God to make
peace with us. It will take all of our might, empowered by the Holy
Spirit, to keep peace with others.

Healthy relationships are not just part of being a Christian; they are
crucial. How can we say we love God, whom we have not seen, if we
cannot love our brother whom we have seen (1 John 4:20)? And Jesus
taught that if we come to the place of prayer and remember that something is not right in a relationship with someone else, we are to leave
religious devotion behind us, make things right with our brother or
sister, and then return to the place of prayer (see Matthew 5:23-24).
God does not want our "religion" if it doesn't radically change the way
we relate to other people in our lives.

Restoring the Image of God

Peacemaking restores the image of God, something of which many Christians have only a vague understanding. Genesis 1:26-27 is an essential statement about the meaning of the image of God:

> Then God said, "Let us make man in our image, in our likeness, and let them rule." So God created man in his own image, in the image of God he created him; male and female he created them.

Notice the multiple references to plurality or community within the Godhead: "Let *us* make man in *our* image, in *our* likeness." This is the Trinity in consultation.

And more, the Hebrew term *elohim*—translated "God" here in Genesis 1:26 and throughout the Old Testament—is, strangely, a plural form, also suggesting the Trinity. *Elohim* literally means "gods." The great, fundamental doctrine of Judaism has always been, "The Lord [YHWH] our God [Elohim], the Lord is one" (Deuteronomy 6:4), and yet the basic Hebrew word for *God* is plural! Christians believe that this is a covert reference to the Trinity in the Old Testament.

In Genesis 1, *Elohim* purposes to create man in His image, in the image of the plurality of His triune Being. The image of the community of the Trinity has been stamped on the community of humanity. The image of God, then, is relationship in community. This is further affirmed in the unusual and often unnoticed statement of Genesis 1:27: "In the image of God he created him; *male and female.*" Or to paraphrase, "In His image *Elohim* created human persons as a community of relational, interdependent beings."

Theologian Millard Erickson writes:

Some would argue that what we have here is a parallelism not merely in the first two, but in all three lines. Thus, "male and female he created them" is equivalent to "So God created man in his own image" and to "in the image of God he created him." On this basis, the image of God in man (generic) is to be found in the fact that man has been created male and female (i.e., plural). This means that the image of God must consist in a unity in plurality.[3]

Peace and Love

This is not to say, of course, that the male-female is the only relationship between two human beings with real meaning. "Male-female" is simply the ultimate model of mutual interdependence and unity in differentiation. In the union of male and female, the two become *one flesh*. The apostle Paul calls this "one flesh" relationship of husband and wife "a great mystery" (Ephesians 5:31-32).

Out of His image God has given us the most precious thing about Himself—the harmonious, loving, consummate oneness He experiences within His own Being. The most sacred thing we have as human beings, outside of our relationship with God, is our relationships with one another. *The image of God is our cohumanity.*

We are mutually dependent on one another, just as there is a mutual dependence among the Persons of the Godhead. No man is an island. God has ordained this forever by permanently imprinting His image of interdependence on us, His special creatures. In all of God's creation, only man fully understands and experiences true relationships. Walter Brueggemann writes:

On the one hand, humankind is a single entity. All human persons stand in solidarity before God. But on the other hand, humankind is a community, male and female. And none is the full image of God alone. Only in community of humankind is God reflected. God is, according to this bold affirmation [Genesis 1:27], not mirrored as an individual, but as a community.[4]

The great biblical term to describe the relational interaction between God and man, and person to person, is *love*. German theologian Otto Weber writes:

> To put it another way, man is in the "image of God" in his predetermination to be one who loves. But he cannot love God without seeing his "neighbor" as destined to be a co-partner in God's covenant and to love him as such. Being-based-upon-God can never be anything other than being-for-the-other-person.[5]

God is love, and love makes peace. God loved the world so much that He gave His only begotten Son to make peace with us (John 3:16). "This is how we know what love is: Jesus Christ laid down his life for us. And we ought to lay down our lives for our brothers" (1 John 3:16).

In terrible contrast, Satan is hate, and hate makes war. It is still his singular purpose to bring strife and division into every level of human society, from the small unit of the home to great international arenas. Our spiritual enemy champions the disruption of relationships. The angels rejoice in heaven when one person is saved. The demons rejoice in hell when a marriage ends in divorce, or when a church is fragmented by strife. Satan's hateful plan is to destroy the thing in us most precious to God—His image.

Created to be a community of love, man has become a world of prejudice and hate. But Jesus "himself is our peace, who has destroyed the barrier, the dividing wall of hostility [between Jews and Gentiles, among everyone].... His purpose was to create in himself one new man out of the two, thus making peace, and in this one body to reconcile both of them to God through the cross, by which he put to death their hostility" (Ephesians 2:14-17).

The great conflict, then, is between Satan and the Prince of Peace, between those who sow strife and those who make peace. As C.S. Lewis wrote in his essay "Christianity and Culture," "there is no neutral ground in the universe: Every square inch, every split second, is claimed by God and counterclaimed by Satan." The image of God, then, will either be tarnished or polished, damaged or restored, based on whether or not we are committed to making and keeping peace.

Readiness

Returning now to Ephesians 6:15, the second important term is *readiness*. Strife and division, the things that erode relationships, seem to occur naturally. You really don't have to look for a fight. One will come your way whether or not you want it. In one of the lesser quoted "promises" of the Bible, Jesus said, "Things that cause people to sin are bound to come" (Luke 17:1). He was not being negative; He was being realistic about life.

Problems just happen; peace doesn't. Peace is elusive. Peace happens because someone makes it happen. Peace is something you have to work on. You have to take the initiative.

If for no other reason, we know this because it is the basic message of the gospel. God Himself took the initiative to make peace. He was in Christ, reconciling the world to Himself (2 Corinthians 5:19), and we have been given the ministry of reconciliation: "Blessed are the peace*makers,* for they will be called sons of God" (Matthew 5:9).

The big question is: How can we *make* peace? How can we be ready?

Many see the Lord's Prayer as a model prayer, a format for daily communion with God. When we pray, "Forgive us our sins, as we forgive others," we prepare ourselves *in advance* for whatever offenses the day ahead may bring. This is just another way to fit our feet with peace.

The key word here is *forgiveness.* We make peace by being prepared to forgive. What separates me from God? Sin. What isolates me from other people? Offenses. What is the correct response? The gospel of peace, forgiveness.

Forgiveness is the power that restores broken relationships between God and man, and man and man. It is because of forgiveness that God accepts me the way I am. Forgiveness opens the door of reconciliation.

Sin separates me from God, but God's forgiveness separates my sin from me, as far as the east is from the west! When God looks at me, He actually sees me without sin. Forgiving others works much the same way. I must release them from what they have done to offend me. When I look at the offender, I must see the person and not the sin.

Impossible? Jesus once told His disciples that forgiveness was absolutely necessary, even if a person sinned against them and repented seven times in one day. Seven times in one day! Most of us can scarcely forgive seven times in a year. When the disciples were confronted with this overwhelming challenge, they cried out in desperation, "Increase our faith!" (see Luke 17:1-5.) The point here is that forgiveness is not a natural human virtue. We need divine intervention and grace to forgive.

No one ever said forgiveness would be easy. In fact, forgiveness comes only through sacrifice. I have to give up something of myself—my anger, my thirst for vengeance, my humiliation, my pride—in order to forgive. Just remember, *Jesus gave up everything.* "Bear with each other and forgive whatever grievances you may have against one another. *Forgive as the Lord forgave you*" (Colossians 3:13).

Forgive we must. Jesus told a parable about a man who refused to forgive a little offense, after his master had forgiven him an insurmountable debt. His master was very angry "and delivered him to the tormentors" (Matthew 18:34, KJV). Emotional torment, even spiritual oppression, is the consequence of unforgiveness, but forgiveness and reconciliation bring peace.

Feet

The third important term in Ephesians 6:15 is *feet.* Frequently in the Bible, the idea of spiritual authority is suggested by the term "feet." This was a common expression of dominion in the ancient world, as a conquering king would literally place his foot on the neck of his vanquished foe.

Psalm 8 states clearly God's purpose for man: to have dominion. Then the psalm declares that God has placed all things "under his feet." The Old Testament predicts that mankind's dominion—God's purpose for Adam and Eve, lost in Eden—will be restored through the coming of the Messiah. He is the One whose foot will crush the head of Satan (see Genesis 3:15).

God the Father says of his Son, "Sit at my right hand until I make your enemies a footstool for your feet" (Psalm 110:1).[6] Using the same figure of speech, Jesus announces to His disciples that they have the authority to walk over serpents, scorpions, and all the power of the enemy (see Luke 10:18-19). The church, as the body of Christ, has everything under her feet as well (see Ephesians 1:22-23).

My conclusion, then, is that "feet fitted with the readiness of the gospel of peace" is a veiled reference to the source of the believer's authority. *There is spiritual authority in peacemaking.* When the devil turns up the heat of hatred, making peace is like aiming a fire hose at a match. There is peace in God's authority, and there is authority in God's peace. Isaiah proclaimed:

> The fruit of righteousness will be peace; the effect of righteousness will be quietness and confidence forever. My people will live in peaceful dwelling places, in secure homes, in undisturbed places of rest. Though hail flattens the forest and the city is leveled completely, how blessed you will be, sowing your seed by every stream.
>
> ISAIAH 32:17-20

Peace at Any Price?

Peace at any price is what counselors call codependency. A woman who is married to an alcoholic, for example, can fall easily into this snare. She is always making excuses for and peace with an angry man who refuses to take responsibility for his own life. She tolerates his behavior and even may think it's really her fault. She may actually allow her husband to brutalize her under the guise of Christian submission.

The cross of Christ was not a doormat. The way of the cross is aggressive self-sacrifice with the singular goal of helping others. In contrast, the way of the world is aggressive self-preservation, which exhibits itself in aggressive behavior.

Codependency (another term is *enmeshment*) never helps anyone. Codependency is loving to be loved. It is loving to meet a need in yourself, instead of loving to meet a need in the other person.

John wrote, "Jesus would not entrust himself to them, for he knew all men" (John 2:24). Jesus did not love in order to get love. He loved because He is love and because we need His love.

The same thing can be said about peacemaking. "Peace at any price" is bought for the sake of my own peace. Peace at any price is like the person with a gun held to his head who shouts, "I'll do *anything* you want if you don't kill me." Jesus calls us to be peacemakers not because peacemaking is a magical way to avoid the pain of life but because it is right.

> Do not repay anyone evil for evil. Be careful to do what is right
> in the eyes of everybody. If it is possible, *as far as it depends on
> you,* live at peace with everyone.
>
> ROMANS 12:17-18

A Prayer for Fitting Your Feet With the Readiness of Peace

Loving Father, thank you that I am at peace with You and that I can come to You confidently because of what Jesus has done. I pray now for peace in my soul—for Your peace, not the false and temporary peace of the world. I pray for the peace that passes all understanding.

I also pray for the strength and grace to be a peacemaker. I will prepare myself now for the unexpected today, tonight, and tomorrow. I forgive—in advance—those who will sin against me. I want to respond in love, not react in anger. I will make every effort to live at peace with everyone.

I resist the Prince of Darkness and his snare of strife. I recognize how destructive strife can be, and I stand against it. I place myself under the lordship of the Prince of Peace. In Jesus' mighty name, Amen.

SIX

The Shield of Faith

In addition to all this, take up the shield of faith, with which you can extinguish all the flaming arrows of the evil one.

EPHESIANS 6:16

L ife is full of flaming arrows. Getting pierced with a sharp object is terrifying enough, but Paul intensifies the image by referring to arrows as being hot as a branding iron. The idea, of course, is derived from the ancient military practice of shooting a barrage of ignited arrows in order to terrorize the enemy and disrupt his ranks. A sure defense was a water-soaked leather shield. Paul calls this the shield of faith.

Without faith it is *impossible* to please God, and without faith it is *impossible* to keep standing in the heat of the battle. Yet at times it seems equally *impossible* to define faith! What is faith?

Elements of Faith

Faith is trust and confidence in another to do what you cannot do yourself. In the Bible, faith means belief and trust in God. Faith, as it is used in the New Testament, has at least four different shades of meaning.

The first of these is *saving faith*. Saving faith is the trust we place in Christ to save us from our sin and its consequences. We are saved by faith in God, not by our works. Faith, in fact, is a renunciation of our own works. It is an attitude that says, "My best righteousness is seriously inadequate."

In what is one of the better-known passages in the New Testament, Paul wrote, "For it is by grace you have been saved, *through faith*—and this not from yourselves, it is the gift of God—not by works, so that no one can boast" (Ephesians 2:8-9). Abraham is a great example of saving faith. He "believed God, and it was credited to him as righteousness" (Romans 4:3).

The second aspect of faith is what I call *faith to receive*. "Without faith," we are told, "it is impossible to please God, and those who come to him must believe he exists and that he is the rewarder of those who diligently seek him" (Hebrews 11:6). In other words, faith makes things happen. Faith produces results. In this sense, faith is our daily trust in God for His help and provision.

Third, the New Testament teaches the need for a special release of faith in particular situations. This is *power faith* or *gift faith* or *miracle-working faith*. The Weymouth translation calls this "special faith" (1 Corinthians 12:9).

It is noteworthy that *faith* is the only term appearing both as a fruit of the Spirit (Galatians 5:22-23) and as a gift of the Spirit (1 Corinthians 12:7-11). This alone should tell us that there are different aspects of faith. It is quite obvious from the teaching of Paul on the spiritual gifts (1 Corinthians 12–14) that not everyone has "power faith" all the time. On the other hand, everyone must have faith in the general sense—faith to be saved and faith to walk with God (Hebrews 11:6).

My fourth category is *enduring faith*. Enduring faith is the kind of faith that does not quit, especially when you feel the most like quitting. Jesus said, "Be faithful, even to the point of death, and I will give you the crown of life" (Revelation 2:10).

The Shield of Faith

The shield of faith is a reference to this last aspect of faith: steadfast-ness and endurance. Why? Because the subject of Ephesians 6 is not salvation, nor is it daily Christian living. Ephesians 6 is about wrestling with the devil. Enduring faith is the persistent, resilient belief that God's Word is true, over and against every problem, wrong thought, or demon.

Enduring faith is wonderfully exemplified by Wycliffe missionaries Pat and Gail Burns, who worked on translating the Bible into the primitive language of Mese. After completing two years of graduate training in linguistics and agreeing to a *fifteen-year* commitment, they relocated, little children and all, to the remote jungles of New Guinea. In one of their monthly newsletters Gail reported:

> [Our daughter] Laura had her first malaria attack, but medica-tion took care of it promptly. It has continued to be unusually, and unseasonably, rainy here, which has caused food shortages for the people. We have requested prayer, and this last week the weather patterns appear to have changed. This letter is being hand-carried out to Lae. Our airstrip has been closed for several weeks, but with improved weather, we are expecting work to be done on it soon so that it can be re-opened. We praise the Lord that we have not had medical emergencies during this time.

Pat and Gail have known a level of sacrifice and commitment few of us will ever experience. They've also encountered unusual spiritual resistance. Theirs is not the "ordinary faith" of daily Christian living, nor is it power faith, although they certainly have needed both of these aspects of faith, too! Instead, their faith has *endured* in the face of uncommon difficulty and intense testing. Their faith has been a shield in the battle. Without it, they could not have survived.

There is no formula for faith in a crisis. Faith is not a magic escape. Enduring faith is a dogged determination to rise above the injustices and pains of life, without allowing the flaming arrows of pain and resentment to penetrate your soul. Life hurts. Faith looks to God and refuses to give those hurts a foothold in your heart.

By faith we are saved. By faith we walk with God. By faith we move mountains. Under the shield of faith, held resolutely above us, we resist the devil and endure the evil day.

Faith and Endurance

"The testing of your faith develops perseverance" (James 1:3). The Greek word translated "perseverance" in this verse is *hupomone*. It is a combination of two Greek words, *meno* and *hupo*, which together mean "to remain under." In the ancient Greek world, the word referred to "a prominent virtue in the sense of courageous endurance," according to Kittel's *Theological Dictionary*. "Distinct from patience," it adds, "it has the active significance of energetic if not necessarily successful resistance." The shield of faith is the ability to remain under the fire of a long, drawn-out trial without breaking down or blowing up.

While writing this book at a Christian retreat center, I met a woman who had been confined to a wheelchair since being shot through the spine in a store robbery in 1971. As she wheeled past my open door, her eye caught me pounding away on my laptop. Turning her chair into my room, she asked me what I was writing.

As we talked, I was surprised at her openness. She had suffered immeasurably, not only from her disability but also because of well-meaning Christians who through the years had dumped on her every imaginable inappropriate comment. She confessed that she had wished the paralyzing bullet had taken her life. And yet there she was, at a Christian retreat, not just surviving but diligently seeking God about her future in full-time Christian ministry.

We are what we decide to be in the face of life's most difficult times. Enduring faith is energetic resistance, no matter what the outcome, no matter how long the devil continues to fire hot darts at our souls. The opposite of enduring faith is short-lived faith, giving up and giving in.

A friend of mine played high school and college football. He told me that one of his team's conditioning drills was to catch automobile tires, rolled down a hill at them by a fiendish coaching staff. It took endurance to face that day after day!

Paul wrote to Timothy, "Endure hardship with us like a good soldier of Christ Jesus" (2 Timothy 2:3). *Endurance* is not a negative or passive word. Endurance is active faith, deflecting persistently the fiery attacks of Satan.

Enduring Faith and the Nature of God

Endurance is godliness, because endurance originates with God. God is the Champion of endurance! God endures from everlasting to everlasting. In Psalm 102:12 we read, "But you, O Lord, sit enthroned forever; your renown endures through all generations."

In one sense, God reigns because God endures. He "survives" every battle, every age, every generation. When you wake up tomorrow morning, God will still be there, and God will still be God. Everything about God endures: His love (Psalm 136), His name (Psalm 72:17), and His Word (Isaiah 40:8).

Jesus is the revelation of God the Father to us, and He, too, is the same yesterday and today and forever (Hebrews 13:8). If you are having difficulty holding up your shield of faith, "consider him who endured such opposition from sinful men, so that you will not grow weary and lose heart" (Hebrews 12:3).

To endure, then, is to reign over life's problems. To quit is to allow life's problems to reign over you.

To endure is to win. The one "who stands firm to the end will be saved" (Matthew 24:13). This refers not just to the inconvenience of a long checkout line at the grocery store or the frustrations of a weekend with the in-laws. Jesus was speaking of enduring in the face of the absolutely worst-case scenario—the fiery days of the Great Tribulation.

How is it possible to endure to the end, especially when the trial seems endless? One day at a time! God has created us with the physical and spiritual capacity to live one day at a time, no more. His mercies are new *every morning.* Give us *this day* our *daily* bread. Take no thought about tomorrow, because there are enough troubles *today.*

There have been times when I have said to myself, "Tomorrow at this time, next week at this time, one year from today, things will be very different. I may not even remember what happened to me today." This is a simple reminder to view life from God's perspective. For Him, a day is like a thousand years, and a thousand years are like a day. The more you enter the eternal, the more you realize the temporality of your problems. Paul knew this:

We do not lose heart. For our light and momentary troubles ["little" things, like being beaten, shipwrecked, imprisoned] are achieving for us an eternal glory that far outweighs them all. So we fix our eyes not on what is seen, but on what is unseen. For what is seen is temporary, but what is unseen is eternal.

2 CORINTHIANS 4:16-18

Weeping may endure for a night, but joy will come in the morning (Psalm 30:5).

The Shield of Faith and the Power of God

First Peter 1:3-9 is a great summary of the concepts in this chapter:

"Through faith [you] are *shielded* by God's power" (verse 5). It is not our faith that shields us; it is God's power. We often speak of the power of faith, but that can be terribly misleading. Our power is not in our faith, *per se,* but in God, who is the object of our faith.

"In *this* [this power of God] you greatly rejoice" (verse 6). I cannot rejoice, precisely speaking, in the troubles of life. No testing *seems* pleasant (see Hebrews 12:11). I rejoice instead in the power of God to shield me and sustain me.

I also rejoice because the troubles of life give my faith an opportunity to grow. Peter continues, "All kinds of trials have come so that your faith—of greater worth than gold, which perishes even though refined by fire—may be proved genuine" (verse 7). Suffering stretches and refines our faith. Difficult times drive us away from self-trust and toward God. The shield of faith is God's power and presence protecting and energizing us in spiritual warfare.

Finally, according to the reading of the King James Version, the shield of faith is "above all" (Greek: "in all"). Faith in the sense of perseverance shields all the other armor. Truth must persevere to prevail. Righteousness must persevere to prevail. We must persevere in peacemaking in order to prevail. And as we will see in the next chapter, every thought becomes obedient to Christ only when we persistently resist the strongholds of the mind.

A Prayer for Holding Up the Shield of Faith

Heavenly Father and mighty God, shield me with Your power as I trust in You. The flaming arrows of the enemy have burned my soul. Heal the pain inside, and give me the strength to resist.

I am committed to enduring to the end of this trial, regardless of how long it lasts. I am not a victim. I am a victor, more than a conqueror through Christ.

My faith, Lord, is in You. I renounce my own abilities, and I confess that unless Jesus builds up my life, everything I do is in vain. Only when I trust You completely am I completely protected from the fiery darts of the wicked one. I hide myself in the fire of Your presence. In Jesus' name, Amen.

SEVEN

The Helmet of Salvation

Take the helmet of salvation.

EPHESIANS 6:17

It was my day off. I was doing some remodeling work at home when the phone rang. I've received my share of kooky calls, but this one deserved an award. The high-pitched, strange voice on the other end of the line asked me if I was Pastor Kinnaman.

"Yes," I answered—warily.

"I need someone to talk to," the voice responded.

Wondering if this was the prelude to a lengthy counseling call, I asked the ambiguous question, "Are you saved?"

"Yes," the voice replied. "I fell into my swimming pool the other day, and someone saved me."

I was speechless. I had never had that kind of response before.

After a short period of silence, the mystery caller began laughing. I realized that my neighbor, who really is saved, was playing a verbal game with my Christian jargon.

Saved may mean any number of things, and a proper definition of *salvation* is necessary if we are to understand "the helmet of salvation."

What Is Salvation?

In the chapter on the breastplate of righteousness, I discussed the difference between "legal" righteousness, which has to do with our eternal standing with God through justification, and "practical" righteousness, our daily walk of obedience as we live out our justification. *Salvation* is another term that has these two aspects.

Salvation—being saved—refers to our release from sin's eternal penalty. Salvation also involves a daily process of change, whereby we grow out of our old patterns of behavior. Not only do I need right standing with God, but my lifestyle needs to change, too, for my sake and for the sake of those around me.

The Greek term has a wide range of meanings, including saving, keeping, benefiting, and preserving the inner being. Salvation, then, is a comprehensive term, most commonly understood as rescue *from* something—namely, sin and its consequences, eternal death and hell on earth.

But salvation is also an endowment, an impartation of divine glory. Salvation is not only an escape; it's a marvelous gift. In the Old Testament, Moses was the great deliverer. He led the people of Israel *out of* Egypt, a symbol of sin and the old life. But Joshua, whose name means "savior," led the people *into* the Promised Land.

Salvation is good news and a grand exchange. With messianic hope, Isaiah wrote:

The Spirit of the Sovereign Lord is on me, because the Lord has anointed me to preach good news [the gospel] to the poor. He has sent me to bind up the brokenhearted, to proclaim freedom for the captives and release [from darkness] for the prisoners, to proclaim the year of the Lord's favor [the year of

Jubilee, figurative of the Messianic Kingdom] and the day of vengeance of our God, to comfort all who mourn,... [and here is the grand exchange:] to bestow on them a crown of beauty instead of ashes, the oil of gladness instead of mourning, and a garment of praise instead of a spirit of despair.

ISAIAH 61:1-3

Not coincidentally, Jesus opened the scroll of Isaiah to this very passage when He introduced His ministry in the synagogue at Nazareth (see Luke 4:14-19). He is the Anointed One, the Messiah, the Christ—the One who makes the grand exchange possible.

The Helmet of Salvation

The term *salvation* is most commonly applied to the soul, as in, "Fourteen *souls* were *saved* last week during our neighborhood evangelistic campaign." Salvation is a change of heart and nature, but it is also a change of mind. *Repentance,* the way to "get saved," is the translation of a compound Greek word, *metanoia,* which means "change of mind" or "change of thinking." Salvation has to do with your head—what you think and how you think.

"Initial" salvation changes my standing with God. The process of salvation changes my thinking, and when I change my thinking patterns, I change my behavior patterns. The apostle Paul wrote to the Romans, "Do not conform any longer to the pattern of this world, but be transformed *by the renewing of your mind*" (12:2). Change your thoughts and you will change your life.

Modern psychology has rediscovered the relationship of thought and behavior. Most notably, psychologist Albert Ellis developed what is known as the rational-emotive theory of human behavior. He identified this behavioral sequence: activating event (*A*), belief (*B*), and consequence (*C*). Most people, he observed, connect *A* and *C* and virtually skip over *B*, as in, "That person [activating event] *makes me* so mad [consequence]."

The fact is, no one *makes* you mad. You make yourself mad. It is what you think, your belief system (*B*), that determines how you feel and react after the activating event. As nationally known motivational speaker John Maxwell has said, "It's not what happens *to* you, it's what happens *in* you."

The fact that we really can control ourselves can be proven from an experience many of us relate to. Have you ever been in a hot argument with someone, your spouse perhaps? And then the telephone rings! For an eternity of silent seconds you stare at each other, wondering who is going to pick up the phone. You do, and it's your boss. Your demeanor changes instantly to cheery politeness! How is it possible for you to be so angry one moment and so gracious the next? Because *you* control your emotions.

My wife and I were having a less than mild disagreement one evening when the doorbell rang. I took a deep breath, put on a mask of self-composure, and opened the door. I was hoping for a salesman so I could quickly resume arguing.

But there stood my brother, grinning at me about his surprise visit. I still remember how my feelings changed, almost instantly. I tried to prevent it, but a smile broke across my face, too. I really was able to control myself. As my thoughts changed, my angry emotions subsided. My wife had not made me angry. I had made myself angry. When I saw my brother, my thoughts changed, which changed my feelings and behavior.

Once I was counseling a young woman who had done some

professional acting. She was facing a serious personal crisis and was not able to control her emotions. So she claimed. I asked her about acting. How was she able to cry when doing a sad part?

"By thinking about a sad time in my life," she answered.

It was exactly the answer I was hoping to hear. "See," I told her triumphantly, "what you think really does affect the way you feel and what you do."

Change your thoughts and your life will change. "Be transformed by the renewing of your mind."

The War in Your Head

Your mind is the battleground of life, and Satan knows that better than any of us. You need the helmet of salvation on your head! Your head needs salvation from wrong thoughts; immoral and impure thoughts; thoughts of suspicion and self-pity; thoughts of anger, hatred, and violence; distorted thoughts; prideful thoughts; obsessive thoughts. Your head needs protection!

David wrote in his most famous psalm, "You anoint my head with oil" (Psalm 23:5). Pouring oil on the head was a common Old Testament practice that symbolized a significant New Testament truth—the anointing of the Spirit. The powerful presence of the Spirit in my life and in my mind brings spiritual victory, as David wrote in the same psalm, "You prepare a table before me *in the presence of my enemies."*

And in Psalm 94:19 we read these lovely, liberating words: "When anxiety was great within me, your consolation brought joy to my soul." A struggle of life and death rages in my mind, and the anointing of God's presence restores my sanity. The mind set on the Spirit brings life and peace.

This is precisely the theme of one of the best known passages in the New Testament on the subject of spiritual warfare, 2 Corinthians 10:3-5. "For though we live in the world, we do not wage war as the world does" (verse 3). In other words, what appears in the natural to be nothing more than a circumstantial problem may in fact have a spiritual cause.

The natural man does not understand the spiritual dimension and looks at life only through the eyes of his body. But the weapons of the Christian "are not the weapons of the world. On the contrary, they have divine power to demolish strongholds" (verse 4). Specifically, these are strongholds of the mind: arguments, pretensions, imaginations, and every thought that is not taken captive to Christ. The mind is a battleground of spiritual strongholds and high places.

The longer I serve in ministry and the more I study spiritual warfare, the more I become convinced that *our thoughts are often influenced by demons.* We need the helmet of salvation not only to save our minds from old patterns of thinking but also to guard our minds against the invasion of demonic influence. Let me explain *how* this happens.

How We Hear "Voices"

Our human nature has two principal aspects: physical and nonphysical. Genesis 2:7 records the creation of the first person: "The Lord God formed man from the dust of the ground [physical] and breathed into his nostrils the breath of life [nonphysical], and man became a living being [that is, fully alive and human]." The physical aspect of our humanity operates through the senses of sight, hearing, taste, touch, and smell. These make us conscious of the physical world around us.

The nonphysical side of our humanity may be further "divided" into soul and spirit (see Hebrews 4:12). The soul is each person's unique personality or self. The Greek word translated "soul" is *psyche,* from which we derive the English word *psychology.* Psychology, simply defined, is the study of the self as the fountainhead of human behavior. The soul may be further defined as mind (what we think), will (what we do), and emotions (what we feel). The mind, as I discussed earlier in this chapter, shapes our actions and feelings.

The other nonphysical part, the spirit, is the human capacity for God and spiritual things. It is the "otherliness" of our humanity.

The body, then, is our world-side, the soul is our self-side, and the spirit is our God-side. Humanity in its fullness is a unique balance and blend of world-consciousness, self-consciousness, and God-consciousness.

I have developed a simple diagram to illustrate this.

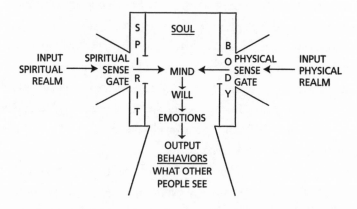

This diagram shows how the soul (mind, will, and emotions) is influenced by "input" from the physical and spiritual dimensions. Once again, the mind is at center stage, because it processes and stores information collected by our physical senses. What happens in our minds depends to a large degree on what we sense physically. If our eyes are blind and our ears deaf, then our minds will be correspondingly blank. People who are visually impaired, for example, rarely, if ever, dream in color, because their eyes have never allowed that kind of information to enter the brain.

Most people do not realize, however, that the "sights and sounds" of the spiritual realm can penetrate our minds just as easily as those of the physical realm. Just as our minds are influenced by what our physical ears hear, our thoughts are influenced by what our spiritual ears are hearing, often subliminally.

This idea of *spiritual* seeing and hearing is, of course, a solidly biblical concept. In the opening chapters of Revelation, for example, Jesus challenged each of the seven churches, "He who has an ear, let him hear what the Spirit says to the churches" (Revelation 2:7).

Another example is the story of Elisha and the siege of Dothan (2 Kings 6:8-22). To ease the fearfulness of his young assistant, Elisha prayed, "O Lord, open his eyes so he may see." At once the young man's eyes were opened, and to his astonishment, he "saw" an incredible display of angelic power encircling and protecting them.

It is possible to see into the spiritual dimension. It may not always be easy, because now in the present we see through a glass darkly (1 Corinthians 12:12). But occasionally the veil lifts and we get a glimpse of true spiritual reality.

Christian believers are not the only ones, however, with a capacity for spiritual things. A person who has not been born again is not necessarily blind: deceived, perhaps, but not dead to spirits and spirituality. Every human being, saved or unsaved, has an intrinsic ability to connect with the spiritual realm, even "hear voices."

This human faculty for spirituality is very real and potentially very dangerous: "The god of this age has blinded the minds of unbelievers, so that they cannot see the light of the gospel of the glory of Christ"

(2 Corinthians 4:4). Unbelievers may have all kinds of spiritual experiences, but they cannot see Christ because of the spiritual power over their minds.

Kurt Koch, well-known worldwide as a lecturer on the occult, is the author of the highly acclaimed book *Christian Counseling and Occultism*. Regarding the power of compulsive thoughts and delusions, he writes:

In the pastoral care of people subjected to occultism we find, besides the psychiatric phenomena, compulsive ideas [thoughts] like fear of mistakes, scruples, compulsions to make vows, to conversion, to confession, to reparation, to doubt and, above all, to blasphemy. Dr. Lechler admits, in the case of the blasphemous compulsion of an emotionally stable person, the further possibility of demonic enslavement.[1]

Human spiritual potential is God-given, but when it is at the mercy of the carnal nature, it is an open door for demonic deception and oppression. Christians differ from other people in that their ears have been opened to the right Spirit: "My sheep listen to *my voice*," Jesus affirmed. "I know them" (John 10:27).

And yet Christians without discernment can be just as readily influenced by "this present darkness." That Christians can be controlled by demons is the thesis of the comprehensive publication *Demon Possession and the Christian: A New Perspective* by C. Fred Dickason, chairman of the theology department at Moody Bible Institute.[2]

Satan's Influence on the Mind

Matthew 16 is probably the best example from the Bible of God's and Satan's direct influence on the human mind.

Jesus queried His disciples, "What are people saying about Me? What have you been hearing?" After a bit of discussion, Jesus turned to Peter and asked: "Who do you say I am?" Peter's famous reply was, "You are the Christ, the Son of the living God" (verse 16).

Listen to Jesus' commentary on Peter's confession: "This was not revealed to you by man, but by my Father in heaven" (verse 17). Jesus made it plain that Peter's spoken thought did not originate in Peter's brain. Peter "heard a voice," the voice of the heavenly Father. It was not an audible voice but a voice spoken in Peter's *spiritual* ear, which caused an unexpected thought in his mind about the identity of Jesus. In the context of the diagram on page 87, spiritual input resulted in behavioral output.

Something else here is highly significant but easily overlooked. Before Jesus specifically identified the source of Peter's thought, *Peter was oblivious to the spiritual dynamics affecting his mind.* He was an unknowing recipient of divine revelation.

In this same chapter, Matthew 16, Peter's mind did a spiritual reversal. When Jesus predicted His death, "Peter took him aside and began to rebuke him, 'Never, Lord!'" (verse 22). Peter was just expressing his concern, he thought, but Jesus again discerned the real source of Peter's "noble idea"—the devil himself! Jesus stunned His disciple with a terrible rebuke: "Out of my sight, Satan!" (verse 23). Again, *Peter was oblivious to the spiritual dynamics affecting his mind.* Clueless, he was an unwitting recipient of spiritual deception.

This is only one of many examples in the Bible of how Satan bends the minds of unsuspecting people. His schemes are elusive and covert.

His work is often difficult to identify, and he will give us every cause to believe that he has nothing to do with how we think—and thus how we feel and act.

Acts 5 records the tragic story of Ananias and Sapphira. The more mature Peter of this event is markedly different from the Peter of Matthew 16. His spiritual discernment has come a long way! Like Jesus, he is not fooled by the devil's methods. He blasts Ananias, "How is it that Satan has so filled your heart³ that you have lied to the Holy Spirit? What made you think of doing such a thing?" (verses 3-4).

Judas was similarly prompted by the devil to betray Jesus (John 13:2). None of these people, I suspect, was fully aware of the power of demons to deceive.

And listen to Paul's warning: "The Spirit clearly says that in later times some will abandon the faith and follow deceiving spirits and things taught by demons" (1 Timothy 4:1). The terrifying thing about this is that people who are in spiritual deception cannot recognize it. They're clueless!

I have never met anyone under religious deception who openly admitted, "I've considered the options, and this is my best choice. I've decided to follow deceiving spirits." Deception is not about picking and choosing ideas that suit your fancy, like buying groceries. It is more like eating cheese from a rat trap. Those who deny the existence of the trap have no inkling that they are in denial, and therein lies the trap's power. Paul wrote, "I am afraid that just as Eve was deceived by the serpent's cunning, *your minds may somehow be led astray* from your sincere and pure devotion to Christ" (2 Corinthians 11:3).

Most of our thoughts are self-initiated. I think most of my own thoughts. But demonic promptings always remain a real and present possibility. The battle rages for our minds. Be totally changed, then, by the renewing of your minds, bringing every thought into captivity to

Christ. Put on the helmet of salvation.

"Whatever is true, whatever is noble, whatever is right, whatever is pure, whatever is lovely, whatever is admirable—if anything is excellent or praiseworthy—think about such things" (Philippians 4:8). "Above all else, guard your heart, for it is the wellspring of life" (Proverbs 4:23).

Discerning the Spirits

How can I guard my thoughts? How can I know where my thoughts are coming from? Discernment is both a gift and a learned skill.

The gift. Paul includes "the ability to distinguish between spirits" in his list of the nine supernatural manifestations of the Holy Spirit in 1 Corinthians 12 (see verse 10). There are three kinds of spirits: evil spirits, human spirits, and heavenly spirits, including angels and the Spirit of God. The discerning of spirits is the ability to identify the kind of spirit behind a particular event, circumstance, or thought. If it is determined that the spirit is an evil one, the discerning of spirits operating with precision can also identify the specific kind of evil spirit.

The skill. Discernment is also a learned skill. The writer of Hebrews describes mature Christians as those "who by constant use have trained themselves to distinguish good from evil" (Hebrews 5:14). Spiritual maturity and wise perception do not develop overnight. There's no getting around it. Sometimes we just have to learn the hard way, chopping a path through the jungle of experience. The only way to get older and wiser is to get older—and wiser!

Thus, remaining teachable and listening to others is paramount, especially when you are young. Paul wrote to the very immature Corinthians, "Even though you have ten thousand guardians in Christ, you do not have many fathers" (1 Corinthians 4:15). Anyone in the church pew will give you advice, and if you ask enough of the "ten thousand" you will always find someone who will tell you what you want to hear.

There are, however, very few spiritual fathers, mature Christians adequately skilled in the Word and in the experiences of life, people who can give you real help. Furthermore, spiritual fathers are willing to make the personal sacrifices necessary to walk you through your problems, unlike the man on the street who, after freely giving you advice about anything, walks away without ever giving you or your problem another thought.

Youth must listen to age. Immaturity must submit itself to maturity (1 Peter 5:5-6), and all of us need to submit to one another (Ephesians 5:21). Every word, every thought, should be tested by two or three witnesses. We guard our minds by submitting our thoughts to one another.

Lastly, we sharpen our discernment skills through the regular practice of the spiritual disciplines. Prayer, fasting, worship, and Bible reading are exercises that strengthen and develop our spiritual senses. The classic book *The Celebration of Discipline,* by Richard Foster (Harper San Francisco), is an excellent guide to understanding the fundamental regimens of the Christian life. Discipline is a price we must pay for the fine-tuning of our spiritual sensitivity.

We must watch carefully and pray fervently. Our adversary the devil prowls about, looking for unsuspecting, undiscerning victims. But as we take up the helmet of salvation and stand in right relationship with God, we will find that Satan's tricks become more obvious and readily combated.

A Prayer for Putting on the Helmet of Salvation

Heavenly Father, forgive me for my wandering thoughts and undisciplined thinking. I realize that I have not been guarding my heart, and I have allowed wrong thoughts to influence and even control me. I resist those thoughts in the name of Jesus, and in the power of His might I cast down every stronghold of wrong thinking: imaginations, pride, self-pity, anger, deceit.

Give me a clear head. Grant me spiritual discernment to recognize the origins of my thoughts. I am committing myself to thinking right and thinking straight. Deliver me from every distortion and misunderstanding.

And, Lord, give me the strength to refrain from speaking my thoughts unless I am certain that what I say will bring honor to You and life to others. I pray this in Jesus' mighty name. Amen.

EIGHT

The Sword of the Spirit

Take the sword of the Spirit, which is the word of God.

EPHESIANS 6:17

I learned a crucial lesson about spiritual warfare the hard way. The year 1987 was the most difficult of my life. The final two months of the year were horrible, and the last week was the worst.

After a long battle with cancer, our church's visitation pastor, Warren Hill, died late in the evening on the last Sunday of 1987. His daughter called me early Monday morning.

Within an hour I picked up the phone again. This time my secretary was calling. In a subdued voice she told me that our receptionist, Bobbi Jo, and her husband, Bob, coming home from a holiday vacation, were in a terrible automobile accident in New Mexico. Bob did not make it. I officiated back-to-back funerals the last two days of December.

All the while, unknown to most of our congregation, I was facing a health crisis myself. During the previous month I had developed a heart problem of unknown cause—at the ripe old age of thirty-eight. I was taking a strong arrhythmia medication, which has since been severely restricted in its application by the FDA. I will never forget the pharmacist's response when I asked about the side effects of the medicine. Staring at the lengthy statement of applications and limitations, he asked me, "Were you on anything else before taking this?"

"No," I replied apprehensively.

"Well," he said, still scrutinizing the document, "this seems to be for when other medication does not work." You can imagine what that did for me.

Things had begun to unravel a few weeks before. I had staggered home one Sunday evening, characteristically exhausted after our four-service Sunday. As I lay in bed, I became aware of a strange sensation in my chest. I checked my pulse. My heart was palpitating erratically, missing a beat every few seconds.

In mild panic, I called the emergency room at the local hospital. They reassured me that my problem as I described it was fairly common, but I had difficulty believing them. I was in good aerobic condition, and I never had had a trace of a heart problem.

The next morning I scheduled an appointment with our family doctor. When I saw him at the end of the day, he arranged a special appointment for me to see a cardiologist immediately. I was given a battery of tests, among them an overnight heart monitor. This last procedure showed that I had six or seven "misfires" every minute, or more than nine thousand irregular beats in a twenty-four-hour period.

The doctor was uncertain of my condition, and I was very frightened. To add to my discouragement, my lifelong friend John was undergoing surgery the same weekend in an attempt to arrest his recently discovered leukemia.

With some of the test results still pending, I decided to get away for a few days to rest and to seek the Lord. When my wife and I returned on Sunday afternoon, my son greeted me with more bad news. That same morning our associate pastor's wife had been in a serious auto accident on the way home from church. She had come within inches of death when her little car was struck at an intersection by a vehicle driven by someone else from our church! It was a miracle that she had survived the crash with only minor injuries.

Her husband, Bob, was preaching at the time of the accident, and one of our ushers interrupted his sermon to give him the news. After courageously finishing his message, he rushed to the hospital to see his wife.

I felt helpless in the hurricane of trouble. The next day I was scheduled to return to the cardiologist for more test results, so I spent the early morning seeking God. You tend to do that when your life is falling apart.

I will never forget the flash of the sword of the Spirit—how God spoke to me and what He said. My Bible literally fell open to Psalm 118, and verses 17 and 18 stood out, seemingly written just for me:

I will not die but live, and will proclaim what the Lord has done. The Lord has chastened me severely, but he has not given me over to death.

My personal journal for that day reads:

God gives me this word: Psalm 118:17-18, at 9 A.M. Dr. appointment at 11. The EKG and X rays are negative. The doctor's prognosis positive. I can even exercise! (In moderation of course, no soccer for a while.) Why all the terrible physical feelings? Doctor does not know. I think nerves. I think the whole thing is stress and spiritual conflict. My faith has not been strong in this fiery trial. I have been very fearful, but God has been faithful.

That was fifteen years ago as of this writing. My heart problem has virtually disappeared, and I haven't had to take medication for years. Our church weathered that season of crisis—and several since. Through it all, we have learned a great deal about wrestling with the devil.

Most significantly, God was faithful to sustain me, to encourage me in His Word, and to stand by His Word. God gave me a liberating, living word, a "sword of the Spirit," to cut through the cloud of emotional spiritual darkness: "I will live and not die."

Let's see how to brandish that sword of the Spirit when the attacks of the enemy and life's tragedies seem to be closing in.

Rhema: The Spoken, Living Word

One Greek term for "word" is *rhema* (plural *rhemata*), which refers to a spoken, living word. Another term, *logos,* is also translated "word," but *logos* has a broader meaning in the sense of truth, ideas, doctrines. Admittedly, *logos* and *rhema* are often used interchangeably in the New Testament, but *rhema* does seem to have its own unique meaning.

According to *A Manual Greek Lexicon of the New Testament,* a *rhema* is a precise spoken word for a specific situation in your life. It is the Bible in its most personal kind of application. The Word of God made alive by the Holy Spirit has spiritual power. Unlike the armor of God for protection and defense, the sword of the Spirit is an offensive weapon for assaulting the strongholds of the enemy.

I like the translation of Ephesians 6:17 in the *New English Bible:* "For a sword, take that which the Spirit gives you—the words that come from God." Spiritual success is not attained by human strength, not even by the power of personal confession. Victory over spiritual darkness is possible only as the Spirit of God undergirds the words we speak. Jesus declared, "The Spirit gives life; the flesh counts for nothing. The words [*rhemata*] I have spoken to you are spirit and they are life" (John 6:63).

The crucial lesson, one we have raised repeatedly in this book, is that you cannot overcome spiritual evil with human effort. For the Christian, the formula for victorious living includes both the Word and the Spirit. Carefully defined doctrines are not enough to defeat the enemy. Even the demons believe what we believe (James 2:19). In fact, Satan's "doctrinal statement" is undoubtedly more accurate and precisely defined than the best systematic theology textbook money can buy.

Certainly it's essential for every Christian to believe the right things about God and Scripture, but the devil is not threatened by correct doctrine alone. No, he flees from the believer who not only stands on the truth of God's Word but also obeys it and is strong in the Spirit. The apostle Paul boasted, "My message and my preaching were not with wise and persuasive words, but with *a demonstration of the Spirit's power*" (1 Corinthians 2:4).

Even Jesus withstood Satan by the Word and the Spirit. Look up the temptation passages, Matthew 4:1-11 and Luke 4:1-13, in a red-letter Bible, which highlights the words of Jesus. Notice how Jesus did not dialogue with the devil. Nor did He rely on superior intellect or even His deity. And unlike so many unequipped Christians, Jesus was not desperately flipping through His concordance for an emergency Bible verse either. Instead He was "full of the Holy Spirit" (Luke 4:1). Satan fled because Jesus spoke God's Word, a timely word and an anointed word, a *rhema.*

Not a Good Doctor...

Imagine visiting a doctor for the first time. During the appointment you discover you are, in fact, his very first patient. New on the job, he is a bit tentative in his diagnosis of your problem. Reaching for his fresh pharmaceutical samples, he prescribes a different pill for each day of the next week, just to make sure he doesn't miss treating one of several illnesses he thinks you *might* have.

Would you ever return to this doctor's office? Or maybe you would want to report him for malpractice.

Certain ailments require a precise diagnosis, followed by a specific prescription. I don't take an antibiotic for a headache, or chemotherapy for a dislocated shoulder. Christian growth and spiritual warfare are no different. I need specific and relevant words from God so I am able to deal with my problems and counter the equally specific schemes of the dominion of darkness.

If you are facing a particularly difficult situation or trying to overcome a temptation or break a habit, you need a *rhema*, a special power word from the Spirit of God. Just reading the Bible or listening to Christian music will not resolve long-term issues. Study the Bible with a purpose. Let the Holy Spirit guide you as you select three or four references that apply specifically to your problem.

Christian psychologist and author Norman Wright recommends a "stop card" to confront your emotions and "just say no." On a three-by-five card, write a spiritual prescription: a Bible verse, or a statement of truth that applies directly to your problem. Carry it with you. When the problem flares up or when the devil comes against you and you feel your emotional self-control slipping, read the card aloud.

I have employed this strategy with great success during the most troubling times in my life. I write down what God has spoken to my heart when I was in a more stable, spiritual frame of mind, like during prayer and fasting or in church. Then, during life's darker moments, I read aloud what God has given me in the light. It works. When Jesus is Lord of my thoughts, I am able to control myself and bind the devil.

How to Receive a *Rhema*

The key is the *rhema*. I don't want to borrow a Bible verse that worked for someone else. I must depend on the "sword of the Spirit, which is the *rhema* of God." If you need a living word, then put this book down now. Spend some time alone with God, and ask for specific divine guidance in your situation.

James put it this way: "Consider it pure joy, my brothers, whenever you face trials of many kinds.... If any of you lacks wisdom, he should ask God" (James 1:2, 5). How to get direction from God (James 1:5-8) is sandwiched between teachings on trials (James 1:1-4) and temptations (James 1:12-15). In other words, James is educating us on how to receive specific guidance from God when we really need help. God *will* give you wisdom, and He won't make you feel guilty about talking with Him honestly about your problems. He really wants to help you.

For James, "wisdom" is practical, not theoretical religious concepts. We frequently (and mistakenly) think of God's wisdom as spiritual ideas and principles, and our favorite question in life is *Why?* But James 1 is not a treatise on the cause of trouble, the *why*. It is, instead, a revelation of *how* to be spiritually successful regardless of the cause of the trial or its ultimate outcome.

When you ask "Why?" as in, "Why did this happen to me?" you probably come up with an answer that does not help you through the trouble. Job had as much trouble as anyone could imagine. He did not need an answer to the *why* question. His friends tried that approach. No, Job needed God.

When wrestling with the devil, a better question than "Why?" is *"How?"* How do I get out of this mess?

Even in the Old Testament, the idea of wisdom is pragmatic. The Hebrew term translated "wisdom" actually refers to the practical skill of a craftsman, not the intellectual wisdom of a scholar. God's wisdom is revealed in His deeds and acts, not in His intellect alone. It is not just what we think intellectually during a spiritual battle that counts; it is what we do.

Concluding the Sermon on the Mount, Jesus told a parable of two men. One built his house on sand, the other on rock. It was the latter whose house withstood the ravages of the storm. And yet the one who built his house on the sand was hardly ignorant! He heard the Word, and perhaps he even understood it. But he did not respond to what he heard. Picking up this same theme, James writes, "Do not merely listen to the word, and so deceive yourselves. *Do what it says"* (James 1:22).

God's wisdom works. When the devil tries to crowd into your life, ask God for wisdom. You can expect a *rhema.*

This is the message of Revelation 12:10-11 as well:

Now have come the salvation and the power and the kingdom of our God, and the authority of his Christ. For the accuser of our brothers, who accuses them before our God day and night, has been hurled down. They overcame him by the blood of the Lamb *and by the word of their testimony.*

Logos is used here, not *rhema,* but the idea of a living, relevant word is clearly implied. The saints overcame the dominion of darkness by the Word of God made real in their own lives—"the *word of their testimony.*"

What I learn from others will stir my faith. What I learn for myself in the crucible of personal experience will change me forever.

John put it this way: "For everyone born of God overcomes the world" (1 John 5:4). Whatever God does will remain: "Once more I will shake not only the earth but also the heavens so that what cannot be shaken may remain" (Hebrews 12:26-27).

Fifteen years ago God gave me a *rhema:* "You will not die, but live." I was severely tested and shaken, but His Word has sustained me.

NINE

The Power of the Spirit

God anointed Jesus of Nazareth with the Holy Spirit and power.
ACTS 10:38

But you will receive power when the Holy Spirit comes on you.
ACTS 1:8

You cannot argue with a demon. Human strength is completely inadequate in spiritual warfare, and the only power that will prevail over the spirit of darkness is the Spirit of God. Spirit must be confronted by Spirit.

What happened to Jesus in this regard should happen to us. The Book of Acts is the story of the people of God receiving what Jesus received—the power of the Spirit—in order to do what Jesus did—prevail in kingdom ministry.

The One baptized in the Spirit at the Jordan River becomes the One who baptizes in the Spirit. Jesus preached the kingdom, did kingdom works, and prevailed over the ancient enemy. The secret of His power was the outpouring of the Holy Spirit. This is a crucial point: *The power of the kingdom of God is the power of the Spirit, and the power of the Spirit is the only way that the kingdom of God will prevail over the kingdom of darkness.*

Jesus and the Spirit: The Christ

The Holy Spirit powered the kingdom ministry of Christ. This theological concept is clearly presented in Luke's Gospel. As prolific writer and theologian Michael Green wrote in *I Believe in the Holy Spirit*, "Luke persistently links the coming of the messianic age with the gift of the Spirit."[1]

Jesus began His public ministry by reading aloud the declaration in Isaiah, "The Spirit of the Lord is on me, because he has anointed me" (Luke 4:18). Matthew highlighted the connection between Jesus and Isaiah's prophecies: "This was to fulfill what was spoken: 'Here is my servant whom I have chosen, the one I love, in whom I delight; I will put my Spirit on him'" (Matthew 12:17-18; see also Isaiah 42:1-4). And in Acts 10:38 we read that "God anointed Jesus of Nazareth with the Holy Spirit and power, and ... he went around doing good and healing all who were under the power of the devil."

The anointing of the Spirit takes us back to the Old Testament practice of anointing with oil, by which Israel's chosen leaders were authorized to represent Jehovah on the earth. Jesus is the consummate prophet, priest, and king, authorized not by oil but by the Spirit, to reestablish the kingdom of God and to overcome the dominion of darkness. Jesus was "the Christ," the anointed One, anointed by the Spirit to do the work of the kingdom.

What happened to Jesus when He was baptized in the Spirit? At least four things.

First, there was a release of kingdom power. When the Spirit authorized Jesus to do the work of the Father, the government of God was placed on Jesus' shoulders (Isaiah 9:6), and demonstrable power was released in His life. As at Pentecost, the Spirit baptism of Jesus was accompanied *and followed* by signs, wonders, and spiritual giftings.

Second, the Spirit brought on Jesus an affirmation of sonship and mission. When Jesus was baptized, the heavens were opened, and a voice said, "You are my Son, whom I love; with you I am well pleased" (Luke 3:22). This was no doubt a reference to the messianic promise of Psalm 2:7: "I will proclaim the decree of the Lord: He said to me, 'You are my Son; today I have become your Father.'"

Jesus was the Son forever (John 1:1), while the Incarnation—the union of deity with humanity—occurred at the moment of His conception in Mary's womb. Jesus knew something of His destiny at the age of twelve, but the full consciousness of His identity, His mission, and certainly the power to fulfill that mission did not occur until His baptism in the Jordan and in the Spirit. The gift of the Spirit descending on Jesus at His baptism was to be understood as a sign of His "official" adoption as Son.

In *Jesus and the Spirit* theologian James Dunn writes, "Out of this confidence that he stood in a specially intimate relation with God arose Jesus' sense of mission. Sonship meant to Jesus not a dignity to be claimed, but a responsibility to be fulfilled" (p. 39). The coming of the Spirit on Jesus was an affirmation of His sonship and mission.

Third, the Spirit baptism of Jesus led almost immediately to spiritual warfare. His hair still wet from the Jordan, Jesus was whisked by the Spirit into the wilderness to confront the Serpent. The coming of the Spirit upon Jesus brought kingdom authority, and an immediate clash of the kingdom of light and the dominion of darkness ensued. Without the coming of the Spirit, this would never have occurred. Satan raises his ugly head only when his dominion is seriously challenged, and his authority is decisively contested when the Holy Spirit is present in power.

Fourth, the coming of the Spirit on Jesus initiated effective ministry. There is no reference in the Scriptures to any public ministry in the life of Christ prior to His baptism in the Spirit. With the exception of the events attending His birth and the story of the boy Jesus in the temple, the New Testament is strangely silent about His childhood years. Only Matthew and Luke mention His birth, but all four Gospels give careful attention to His baptism. The baptism of Christ is the crucial starting point for His public ministry and, for that matter, all of the New Testament that follows.

It is significant that the Gospel writers focus almost exclusively on the ministry words and works of Jesus *after* He received the Spirit. The coming of the Spirit upon Jesus resulted in kingdom authority, by which Jesus overcame the devil and began effective public ministry. Effective public ministry means that the kingdom of Christ is overcoming the dominion of darkness. Jesus was "the Christ," the anointed One, anointed by the Spirit to do the work of the kingdom.

Christians and the Spirit: Anointed Ones

The Spirit baptism of Jesus was intended to be a model experience for every Christian. "Christ-ians" are "anointed ones" ("little Christs"), just as Jesus was the Anointed One, the Christ. Our natures differ. Jesus was God incarnate, but the Spirit who came upon Him is the same Spirit in whom He baptizes believers to be His witnesses and to do His work.

Thomas Smail wrote in *Reflected Glory*, "In both Christ and us the Spirit is working with the stuff of our common humanity; because He is man and we are men, it becomes possible and credible that what the Spirit did in Him, He should be able to do again in us" (p. 63). We have examined what the Spirit did in Jesus. Let's see what happens when the Spirit comes on us.

First, He releases kingdom authority and power in us. Jesus has transferred His authority to the church. The Great Commission to go into all the world is entirely dependent on the premise that appears in the preceding verse: "All authority in heaven and on earth has been given to me. Therefore go" (Matthew 28:18-19). Jesus is commissioning us to make disciples in the context of the restoration of God's authority in a godless and demonized world. It is clear in the other Great Commission accounts in Luke, Acts, and Mark that the power of which Jesus speaks—authority in heaven and in earth—is none other than the Pentecostal outpouring of the Holy Spirit.

In Luke's account of the Great Commission, both in his Gospel and in Acts, Jesus expects His disciples to wait in Jerusalem for the coming of the Spirit's power (Luke 24:48-49; Acts 1:8). And Mark predicts that powerful signs and wonders will follow those who respond in faith to the Great Commission (Mark 16:15-18). Even though some dispute the textual validity of this last chapter in Mark, it certainly demonstrates the belief of the early Cchurch: To be empowered by the same Spirit that came upon Jesus is to do the works of power Jesus did.

Second, when the Holy Spirit comes upon Christians there is a special affirmation of sonship and mission. When Jesus received the Spirit, a voice from heaven proclaimed His unique relationship with the heavenly Father and what that union meant in terms of God's mission for His life. Something very similar occurs when the Spirit comes upon the believer.

"For you did not receive a spirit that makes you a slave again to fear, *but you received the Spirit of sonship.* And by him we cry, 'Abba, Father.' The Spirit himself testifies with our spirit *that we are God's children*" (Romans 8:15-16). Those who have been Spirit-baptized have a deep and certain consciousness of their union with God, and their accompanying destiny: the kingdom commission. Just look at what happened to the disciples when the Spirit came at Pentecost!

Third, Holy Spirit baptism is a declaration of war. Immediately after His baptism, Jesus was led by the Spirit into the desert to confront the ancient Serpent in a kind of replay of Eden. The setting and players were different, but the devil's strategy was the same: to keep the world under his authority, not God's. Jesus did not succumb, however, showing us that the empowering of the Spirit also enables the believer to be victorious in the conflict of the kingdoms, to rule and reign with Christ over the powers of darkness. Kingdom authority is released by the power of the Holy Spirit.

In a kind of pre-Pentecost training exercise, Jesus commissioned seventy of His disciples to announce the kingdom and to heal the sick. When they returned and recounted the dramatic signs that had accompanied their ministry, Jesus told them that he had "seen" something in the Spirit. He had seen Satan fall from heaven like a bolt of lightning, to which He added this significant comment: "I have given you authority to tread upon serpents and scorpions, and over all the power of the enemy" (Luke 10:19, NAS).

We find this same theme in Ephesians 1:18-29, where Paul prays for his followers, that the eyes of their hearts may be enlightened in order to know "the incomparably great power for us who believe." It is that same power of the Spirit that raised Christ from the dead (see Romans 8:11) and established Him as the Head of the church over all "rule and authority, power and dominion not only in the present age but also in the one to come" (Ephesians 1:21).

The theme of Ephesians is the church and her heavenly warfare (see Ephesians 6:10-18). Like Jesus, believers must receive the Spirit to triumph over Satan. Only by the fire of the Spirit can we overcome the power of hell!

Fourth, when the Spirit comes upon Christians, He launches the church into powerful public ministry. For Jesus, public ministry was not limited to speaking out on religious or social issues. When the Spirit came on Jesus, signs of the kingdom followed. He preached great messages, but miracles confirmed the word. The same thing happened when the Spirit came upon the church in the Book of Acts. The power of the Spirit transformed a small, reclusive band of quivering disciples into a spiritual army that turned the world upside-down.

The Spirit Within and Upon

It is important to make a distinction between the two principal aspects of the work of the Spirit. On the one hand, the New Testament clearly teaches the concept of the Spirit's dwelling *within* the believer. This aspect of the Spirit's work produces the *fruit* listed in Galatians 5:22-23 (love, joy, peace, longsuffering, and so on). On the other hand, the Spirit's work that I have been developing in this chapter involves the release of *kingdom power and ministry gifts upon* the believer. The Spirit *within* develops our character; the Spirit *upon* releases ministry. I diagram it this way:

Spirit Within ⟶ Fruit ⟶ Maturity
Spirit Upon ⟶ Gifts ⟶ Ministry

Jesus is a prototype for every believer. He was conceived by the Holy Spirit (born of the Spirit, we could say), God made flesh. Like Jesus, we become partakers of the divine nature through spiritual birth (see 1 Peter 1:4). The difference, of course, is that Jesus had no sin nature. He was conceived and birthed by the Spirit, not born again.

As a consequence of the nature and Spirit of God *within* Him, Jesus grew in wisdom and in favor with God and man (Luke 2:52), but this alone was not enough to qualify Him for leadership. Nor did it prepare Him for kingdom ministry and spiritual warfare.

It was not until the Holy Spirit came *upon* Jesus that He began His power ministry. He affirmed His calling on the basis of the Spirit *upon* Him, not His wonderful, godly life (the Spirit *within* Him). In *Secret Power* the great evangelist D.L. Moody wrote:

> The Holy Spirit dwelling in us is one thing: I think this is clearly brought out in Scripture; and the Holy Spirit upon us for service is another thing. Every believer has the Holy Ghost dwelling in him. He may be quenching the Spirit of God, and he may not glorify God as he should, but if he is a believer on the Lord Jesus Christ, the Holy Ghost dwells in him. But though Christian men and women have the Holy Spirit dwelling in them, yet He is not dwelling within them in power; in other words, God has a great many sons and daughters without power. Then, the Holy Spirit in us is one thing, and the Holy Spirit on us is another. (pp. 33-48)

Christians today commonly fail to make this distinction. On the one hand some believe we receive all of the Spirit at the moment of salvation. This view generally overlooks the need for power ministry as exemplified by Jesus and the early church. It also explains how Christians can be mature yet seem to lack spiritual power.

On the other hand, I have heard people say, "I need the outpouring of the Spirit's power so I can live a more consistent Christian life." As I understand the Bible, the Pentecostal experience of the Holy Spirit does not make a person a better Christian. Even Jesus, when He received the Spirit, when He was baptized, did not become "better" in the quality of His life.

Paul affirms this same principle in his First Letter to the

Corinthians, who excelled in the power gifts but lacked basic Christian virtues. This explains how Christians can be very gifted and yet immature at the same time.

Godliness is not born in a charismatic moment. It results from decades of disciplined obedience to the Scriptures. Jesus submitted to the Father and learned the Scriptures for thirty years. Only then did the Father anoint him for ministry. The outpouring of the Spirit on Jesus authorized and empowered Him to do the works of the kingdom. Now Jesus baptizes us in the same Spirit, authorizing and empowering us to do the work of the kingdom.

The Spirit and the Spiritual Realm

When the Spirit comes in power, He opens the door to the spiritual realm. When the Spirit came upon Jesus, "heaven was opened" (Luke 3:21). Not surprisingly, we see a parallel in the Book of Acts. On the Day of Pentecost the heavens were opened again. The text of Peter's Pentecost sermon was this well-known passage from Joel's prophecy:

> In the last days, God says, I will pour out my Spirit on all people. [Notice the results:] Your sons and daughters *will prophesy,* your young men will *see visions,* your old men will *dream dreams.* I will pour out my Spirit in those days, and they will *prophesy.*
> ACTS 2:17-18

The prophets of old were called "seers" because they could see into the invisible, spiritual realm. This is precisely what happens when the Holy Spirit comes upon believers. I refer again to the diagram in Chapter 7, to which I have added the entrance of the Spirit's power.

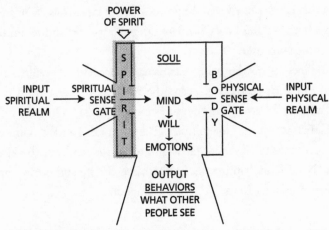

The Spirit lifts the curtain on the stage of the spiritual dimension and gives us the power to overcome the spirits of darkness. Our knowledge and prophecy are partial (1 Corinthians 13:9). We do not "see" the whole picture, but if the Spirit does not open up the heavens, we will not see anything at all.

This may have been Paul's reason for writing, "Eagerly desire spiritual gifts, *especially the gift of prophecy*" (1 Corinthians 14:1). Why? Because prophecy penetrates the invisible spiritual dimension: "The secrets of [a person's] heart will be laid bare. So he will fall down and worship God, exclaiming, 'God is really among you!'" (1 Corinthians 14:25). Prophecy "sees" and discerns, and the coming of the Spirit makes that happen. Prophecy, then, is a primary spiritual gift.

All the supernatural gifts, however, are significant because they reach beyond what is natural and visible. The spiritual gifts are not just charismatic entertainment. They are expressions of the only kind of power capable of overcoming the dominion of darkness. If they were necessary in the life of Jesus and the early church, they are essential in the life of the believer today.

TEN

Binding and Loosing

Whatever you bind on earth will be bound in heaven, and whatever you loose on earth will be loosed in heaven.

MATTHEW 18:18

Our family evening meal was about to begin. I asked our four-year-old son to thank God for the food. As he muttered some disconnected words about Jesus and dinner, I opened one eye and caught him contorting his face in a particularly religious fashion.

I wanted to tell him, "You don't have to make funny faces to get God to listen to your prayers." And then it hit me. He was innocently mimicking his parents! I wanted to repent!

When I first witnessed power ministry, I prayed the way I heard others pray. Like the sons of Sceva (Acts 19:13-20), I rebuked demons the way I heard others rebuke them. I was even careful about my inflection. After all, if you are binding the devil, you have to do it with a voice that sounds authoritative. Or so I thought.

"I bind you, devil!" When you hear people say this, do you know what they mean? Do *they* know what they mean?

I get the impression that for many believers, binding and loosing are a kind of Christian abracadabra. For others, it's empty charismatic chatter. Like when I'm turning steaks on the grill and the direction of the breeze shifts slightly. Reacting to the smoke in my eyes, I yell out,

"I bind you, smoke!" My friends around me laugh, and one of them blurts out, "Praise the Lord!" Sometimes we are just way too casual about our spirituality.

Confronting demons is a grave business and, at times, highly complex. Binding and loosing are not spiritual magic. They have to do with the authority of the Christian in spiritual warfare, and there are often many factors involved. Simply defined, binding and loosing are confident assurance and confession of God's order and government over against the disorder of a sin-cursed, demonized world. But there is also much more.

Binding, Loosing, and the Great Commission

In what is commonly known as the Great Commission, Jesus announced that He had been given *all* authority *in heaven and on the earth* (Matthew 28:18). Notice the parallel with our opening verse: "Whatever you bind *on earth* will be bound *in heaven,* and whatever you loose *on earth* will be loosed *in heaven"* (Matthew 18:18). Jesus has transferred and imparted His authority and power to the believer.

When we pray, "Your kingdom come. Your will be done, on earth as it is in heaven," we are releasing the authority of Christ. Christians have the right and the responsibility to pray for change whenever anything is not under the lordship of Christ.

Jesus came into the world as the firstfruits of God's purpose for His new humanity. The Spirit of the Lord was *upon* Him. He was authorized to "proclaim freedom for the prisoners, to release the oppressed, to proclaim the year of the Lord's favor" (Luke 4:18-19).

As Jesus lived it, this was not a reference to political or social liberation. The world's problems have never been primarily political or social but spiritual, and this was the thrust of Jesus' ministry as He fulfilled the prophecy of Isaiah 61. "To release the oppressed" meant casting out the evil spirits that were holding people captive. It's striking that the first miracle recorded by Luke, immediately after Jesus' messianic declaration in Nazareth, was an exorcism (Luke 4:31-37).

Even John the Baptist, expecting a Messiah who would bring political and social reform, started to question Jesus' ministry. While he was in prison, he sent his disciples to ask, "Are you the one who was to come, or should we expect someone else?" Jesus replied, "Go back and report to John what you hear and see: The blind receive sight, the lame walk, those who have leprosy are cured, the deaf hear, the dead are raised, and the good news is preached to the poor" (Matthew 11:3-5). Jesus was a great social reformer, but He taught that permanent changes in people and society must begin in the spiritual realm.

Binding, Loosing, and the Finished Work of Christ

Quoting Psalm 68:18, the apostle Paul declared that the risen Christ "led captivity captive" (Ephesians 4:8, KJV). The classic Bible expositor Matthew Henry wrote of this verse, "He conquered those who conquered us." Jesus is Lord, seated at the right hand of the throne of God, "far above all rule and authority, power and dominion, and every title that can be given, not only in the present age [on the earth] but also in the one to come [in heaven]" (Ephesians 1:21). God has placed all things under His feet.

Christ has transferred His authority to us so that we can represent Him on the earth. On the bedrock of His finished work and limitless spiritual authority, Jesus *will* build His church. It was God's eternal purpose "that now [in this age, on the earth], *through the church,*

[God's] manifold wisdom should be made known to the rulers and authorities in the heavenly realms" (Ephesians 3:10). In anticipation of His complete victory, Jesus proclaimed that the gates of Hades will not prevail or stand against the church (Matthew 16:18).

The gates of ancient cities were entrance points into the hearts and lives of the people who lived there. It was common for the city fathers to conduct business and pass laws at the gates. Gates, then, took on a symbolic significance; so the phrase "the gates of hell" points to the authority and counsels of the dominion of darkness. In other words, the counsel of hell will not prevail over the purposes of God, and God will fulfill His plan through the church.

In this context Jesus also promised, "I will give you the keys of the kingdom of heaven; whatever you bind on earth will be bound in heaven, and whatever you loose on earth will be loosed in heaven" (Matthew 16:19).

Binding and Loosing in Spiritual Warfare

The use of the phrase *binding and loosing* did not, in fact, originate with Jesus. It was a frequent expression of first-century Jewish rabbinical teaching. According to Alexander Bruce in *The Expositor's Greek Testament*, to bind and loose (Greek: *deo* and *luo*) meant simply "to prohibit and to permit," that is, to establish rules.[1] The Jewish religious authorities at the time of Christ retained the right to establish guidelines for, or keys to, religious practice and social interaction.[2]

But *deo* (to bind, tie) also expresses supernatural control. In Luke 13:15-16, Jesus rebuked a Jewish leader:

You hypocrites! Doesn't each of you on the Sabbath untie [Greek: *luo*, loose] his ox or donkey from the stall and lead it out to give it water? Then should not this woman, a daughter of Abraham, whom Satan has kept bound [Greek: *deo*, bind] for eighteen long years, be set free [Greek: *luo*, loose] on the Sabbath day from what bound her?

Binding and loosing is an activity of spiritual warfare. Satan himself will be bound (Greek: *deo*) with a great chain (Revelation 20:1-2). The conservative *New International Dictionary of New Testament Theology* admits cautiously:

The idea of binding may also refer back to the picture of the binding of the strong man (that is, Satan) who must first be bound (the same verb, *deo*) before his goods (that is, those enthralled by him) may be plundered (Matthew 12:29, parallel Mark 3:27; see also Luke 11:21 which does not use [the same Greek] word). Thus Peter would be promised the power that Christ had to bind the powers of evil and to liberate men, and this would hold good not only on earth, but also in heaven.[3]

Binding and Loosing and God's Will

In a previous chapter I discussed the plural *you* used throughout the New Testament. Matthew 16:18 is an exception, where Jesus speaks directly to Peter about the gates of Hades: "Whatever *you* (singular) bind on earth ..." In this sense, every individual believer has the right and responsibility to resist the devil. You, individually, will be singled out and challenged by spirits of darkness, and you, personally, must resist temptation, restrain yourself, and stand your ground.

The same command to bind and loose, however, is also recorded two chapters later (Matthew 18:18). This time the *you* Jesus uses is plural. Binding and loosing devils, particularly higher levels of spiritual dominion, is not something you should tackle on your own.

My friend Al Ells, a Christian psychologist and author, recounted to me an unusual story abut the danger of what I call indiscriminate binding and loosing. On his way to a meeting in downtown Phoenix, Al heard a radio news report of a recent court decision that struck him as decidedly humanistic. Indignant and angry, Al began to rebuke the principality behind the organization responsible for bringing the issue before the court.

In a flash, Al had a vision of a huge, dark spirit reacting to the arrow of his prayer as it pierced its side. But it was a mini-arrow, and the giant spirit in the vision reacted violently, striking Al on the face. Al began immediately to experience intense pain on the right side of his head.

It was not until later in the day, when he received prayer from his counseling center staff, that he was released from the pain. Al learned an important lesson about spiritual warfare: He had challenged a significant dark power outside the boundary of his authority. Al was binding and loosing out of his anger, not out of the clear will of God.

Jesus implies this need for caution in His command to bind and loose. A more precise translation of the Greek text of Matthew 16:19 and 18:18 is: "Whatever you bind on earth *will already have been bound* in heaven, and whatever you loose on earth *will already have been loosed* in heaven."[4] In other words, binding and loosing must always be in the will of God for a particular situation.

A.T. Robertson, a widely recognized New Testament scholar, comments on Matthew 16:19 in *Word Pictures in the New Testament,* "All of this [that is, the unique grammatical construction in the Greek text] assumes, of course, that Peter's use of the keys will be in accord with the teaching and mind of Christ."[5]

After I preached on this subject once, a woman in our church sent me this remarkable testimony, which I relay here with her permission:

> Several months ago I went over to [a Christian friend's] to pray through her house. I thought I was doing the "right thing," as there had been many problems in their home and marriage. However, I never stopped to ask the Lord if I *should* go. We prayed, did warfare, pulling down strongholds, and went home. I was *physically* spent, so tired that I had to lie down for a nap. I didn't even want to talk to anyone.
>
> That night something happened. We awoke at 5:30 A.M. to find our house flooded with water! When we asked the Lord what had happened, He said, "You stirred up a hornet's nest, and this is the result of it." He revealed how I did not even ask Him if I should have "cleaned" my friend's house. Her husband was not in agreement, and it was not God's will for me to do warfare there.
>
> There were things God wanted accomplished in that family's order of things that I had interfered with. Well, the Lord took care of the damage [of the water-soaked house], and we learned an important lesson—to be obedient to the Lord, our Commander and Chief.

Jesus commissions us to bind and loose, but we dare not do it indiscriminately, whenever we have the urge. Spiritual warfare is serious business. Concerned about His disciples' carnal elation over their newfound spiritual power, Jesus cautioned them, "Do not rejoice that the spirits submit to you, but rejoice that your names are written in heaven" (Luke 10:20).

We cannot expect to beat on the devil whenever we have the whim. But when we are called to act—such as joining in prayer in a deliverance session for another—we can do so with the knowledge that our words carry authority.

Binding, Loosing, and the Authority of the Church

We need to pray and intercede. We need to resist Satan, and he will flee from us. But attacking him directly is another matter. We must know our spiritual jurisdiction, and if we are dealing with a particularly powerful principality, then we need the support and agreement of other praying saints. This leads me to my next point: Binding and loosing are directly related to the order and authority of the church.

The hierarchy of darkness understands authority and chain of command far better than God's people. This is why rebellion or an attitude of independence in us can be so dangerous. If our hearts are not dependent on God, then we are vying for His authority in our lives. Thus we are to rely on God's authority, not our own, in order to rebuke the works of Satan.

Jude's little epistle is a stinging rebuke of those who arrogantly "reject authority and slander celestial beings" (verse 8). To illustrate, Jude adds, "Even the archangel Michael did not dare to bring a slanderous accusation against [the devil], but said, 'The Lord rebuke you!'" (verse 9). We cannot operate from God's authority and our own at the same time. A house divided against itself cannot stand. Anarchy in my heart will never overcome a carefully structured hierarchy in hell.

It is not by accident, then, that the binding and loosing commission of Matthew 18:18 is preceded by instructions on authority and discipline in the church (verses 15-17) and is followed by the promise:

If two of you on *earth* agree about anything you [plural] ask for, it will be done for you [plural] by my Father in *heaven* [note the references to "earth" and "heaven," parallel with verse 18]. For where *two or three* come together in my name, there am I with them.

MATTHEW 18:19-20

The community of other believers provides a protective covering for us.

The fellowship of the saints is also a place of accountability. If there is sin in the church, we have the responsibility to confront people with love and restore them with gentleness: "If your brother sins against you, go and show him his fault, just between the two of you" (Matthew 18:15; see also Galatians 6:1). Sin is a doorway for the devil, and mutual accountability is a shelter in the spiritual storm.

An open and trusting relationship with another believer is like a mirror. Others allow me to see myself more clearly, if I am willing to look and listen. Just as "friends do not let friends drive drunk," so Christian friends do not let Christian friends come under the influence and dominion of darkness. A friend a day keeps the devil away. In other words, effective binding and loosing depend on the quality of our relationships with one another in the body of Christ. One soldier cannot win a war; it takes an army.

Binding and Loosing and a Spirit of Forgiveness

We have looked at binding and loosing from the standpoint of spiritual warfare—binding the devil's power—but I should also mention that there is a type of binding and loosing that can occur in relationships with fellow Christians. This has to do with forgiveness.

Open relationships work two ways: I must be open to correction and receiving forgiveness, and I must correct and forgive. To bind is to withhold forgiveness and redemption; to loose is to give it freely. In John's Gospel, Jesus gave the binding-loosing commission this relational twist: "If you forgive anyone his sins, they are forgiven; if you do not forgive them, they are not forgiven" (John 20:23).

The Greek word here translated "forgive" means "to release" and is a synonym of *luo* ("to loose"). Many Greek authorities believe that John 20:23 is parallel with Matthew 16:19 and 18:18. Forgiveness looses the one who offends you from the guilt and penalty of your anger. Forgiveness is freedom. Unforgiveness binds both the unforgiving one and the unforgiven one. Unforgiveness is torment (Matthew 18:34).

Notice that Jesus told the parable of the unforgiving man (Matthew 18:22-35) in response to Peter's question, "How many times shall I forgive my brother when he sins against me?" (Matthew 18:21). And Peter asked the question so Jesus would clarify what He had just said about church discipline, binding and loosing, and the power of spiritual unity in prayer. Binding and loosing of the powers of darkness is ineffective without the spirit of forgiveness.

In summary, how do we bind and loose? What are the keys of the kingdom? They are the finished work of Christ, seeking God's will, submission to the authority of the church, and a spirit of forgiveness. If you feel these "conditions" are met, then you can speak rebuke to the devil and bind his evil power as the Lord leads you.

We will learn more about binding and loosing by the prayers we pray and by the praise we offer to God, two crucial topics to which I have devoted the final chapters of this book. But first let's look at demonization and ways to accomplish deliverance.

ELEVEN

Demonization and Deliverance

*And these signs will accompany those who believe: In my name they
will drive out demons.*

MARK 16:17

I was teaching a large group of people in a week-long discipleship
school. My subjects were the gifts of the Spirit and the power of God.
To supplement the lectures, I scheduled a spiritual gifts clinic one
evening to demonstrate the reality and practice of the gifts.

The special presence of God was quite evident. A number of
people asked for prayer, among them a young woman who had serious emotional problems. As I began to pray for her, she fell suddenly
to the floor in what appeared to be a seizure.

It seemed to me that her problem was demonic, so I commanded
the spirit to release her. Her body relaxed, and she began to cry. The
next day she testified of the dramatic change that had happened in her
life. Her countenance was noticeably transformed, and many of the
people in the school who knew her well confirmed that she was acting
like a different person.

Even though exorcism was a common feature of Jesus' ministry, the
notion of demon possession is foreign to many Christians. But as Fred
Dickason writes in *Demon Possession and the Christian,* "The New
Testament and current events demonstrate the truth of demon invasion and control of humans."[1]

Matthew and Dennis Linn have taught on healing in many countries and universities, including a course that is part of a doctor's degree accredited by the American Medical Association. In the introduction to their book *Deliverance Prayer*, Matthew Linn confesses his previous struggle to believe in the reality of demons today:

> Ten years ago I could not have edited this book. I knew that Christ called us to preach, heal and cast out demons in his name (Mark 6:12-13; 16:15-18). I was willing to do the first two but didn't believe at all in demons. My graduate studies in anthropology, psychology and theology convinced me that demons were only to be found as gargoyles on medieval cathedrals or fantasies created by too much demon rum....
>
> A growing number of doctors, psychiatrists and social workers now know that it is sometimes as necessary to treat demonic bondage with deliverance prayer as it is to treat bacteria with penicillin, a manic depressive neurosis with therapy and drugs, or an alcoholic with AA and environmental change.
>
> Through the Association of Christian Therapists I have come to know over twelve hundred professionals who combine healing power, of which deliverance is a small but important part, with their professional practice.[2]

Jesus and Demons

If we believe that Jesus was God in the flesh, then we are bound to accept His worldview, including His sensitivity to demon domination of human lives. Otherwise, we are left with a Jesus who was unwittingly influenced by primitive superstitions, an ignorant Jesus who is less than God, as some have actually believed. But to believe in Jesus is to believe in what He said and what He did, and a significant component of His ministry was healing demon-possessed people.[3] Perhaps Matthew summarizes it best:

> Jesus went throughout Galilee, teaching in their synagogues, preaching the good news of the kingdom, and healing every disease and sickness among the people. News about him spread all over Syria, and people brought to him all who were ill with various diseases, those suffering severe pain, *the demon-possessed,* the epileptics and the paralytics, and he healed them.
>
> MATTHEW 4:23-24

Jesus believed that demons play a significant role in human behavior and that they must be driven out.

Demonization

Demons are elusive, but demons are real. They even have the ability to enter the life of a human being. Intertwining themselves with the personality of their victim, demons can control to one degree or another various aspects of the person's life. Dickason defines demonization as "demon-caused passivity or control due to a demon's residing within a person, which manifests its effects in various physical and mental disorders and in varying degrees."[4]

Using the story of the Gerasene demoniac in Mark 5, Kurt Koch, the theologian who wrote *Occult Bondage and Deliverance* with psychiatrist Alfred Lechler, has identified eight distinct symptoms of demon possession:

1. The man was actually indwelt by another being (verse 2).
2. He had unusual physical strength (verse 3).
3. The possessed man had fits of rage (verse 4).
4. The fourth symptom is split personality. The demoniac ran to Jesus for help yet cried out in fear (verses 6-7).
5. The man was resistant to the Christian faith and to spiritual ministry (verse 7). Koch notes here that "one meets this resistance to spiritual help quite often in counseling [demonized] people" (p. 58).
6. The sixth symptom is clairvoyant power. The possessed man knew immediately who Jesus really was (verse 7).
7. The man demonstrated a variation or alteration of voice. A "legion" of demons spoke out of him (verse 9).
8. The eighth characteristic is occult transference (verse 13).[5]

Demons and Christians

Fr. Michael Scanlan, president of Franciscan University of Steubenville (Ohio), and coauthor Randall J. Cirner have identified in *Deliverance from Evil Spirits* three ways that demons affect human persons: temptation, opposition and bondage.[6] We have seen how the dominion of darkness tempts and opposes the saints. As we noted, the apostle Peter warns us, "Be self-controlled and alert. Your enemy the devil [that is, the enemy of Christian believers] prowls around like a roaring lion looking for someone to devour. Resist him" (1 Peter 5:8-9).

A controversial question, however, has to do with the other way evil spirits affect people: Can a Christian be demon-possessed? The debate among Christians over this question will probably never be resolved, because the Bible does not address the question directly. Yet I believe it is possible for a Christian to be demonized.[7] I think the woman

mentioned at the beginning of this chapter and others I have minis-
tered to have been bound by demonic power. In her classic 1912 work
on demons, *War on the Saints,* Jessie Penn-Lewis purports:

> Christians are as open to possession by evil spirits as other men,
> and become possessed because they have, in most cases, *unwit-
> tingly fulfilled the conditions upon which evil spirits work.* The pri-
> mary cause of deception and possession in surrendered believers
> may be condensed into one word, PASSIVITY: that is, a cessa-
> tion of the active exercise of the will in control over spirit, soul
> and body.[8]

As I wrote in a previous chapter, I learned about the reality and power
of demons the hard way. Our whole church was a target, and I was the
bull's-eye. I have never experienced such powerful oppression and spiritual torment. There were times when some of us could "feel" a presence enter our church offices. An invisible cloud of dark resistance frequently visited our staff and elder prayer meetings.

Personally, I battled obsessive thoughts, especially about the validity
of God's call on my life, and at times I was convinced God had aban-
doned me. But God gave me great grace, and with all the temptations
He gave me a way of escape. With the help of family and friends I was
able to endure (see 1 Corinthians 10:13). Was I demonized? I don't
believe so, although the dominion of darkness had enormous influence over my thoughts and feelings during that season of my life.

Perhaps no one has done a more thorough investigation of this subject than C. Fred Dickason. After a comprehensive study of Scripture,
clinical considerations, and an analysis of case studies, Dickason concludes, "We must allow the distinct probability that biblically guided
investigation and counsel has shown in experience that Christians have

been demonized. The evidence is heavily weighted toward that conclusion."[9]

Deliverance

If demons inhabit people, then deliverance is a necessary aspect of
Christian ministry. "And these signs will accompany those who
believe: In my name they will drive out demons" (Mark 16:17).
Scanlan and Cirner suggest several types of deliverance.[10]

Personal or self-deliverance is often possible through significant
growth in personal holiness, or a person might minister to himself by
commanding the evil spirits to leave in the name of Jesus.

Fraternal deliverance is when God works through Christian brothers and sisters to minister release from spiritual oppression.

The third type is *pastoral deliverance.* "When a person has pastoral
responsibility for other people, the Lord gives that person the gifts and
the authority to deal with deeper and more complex workings of evil
spirits."

Fourth is *special ministry.* "God has given to some people special
gifts of discernment, revelation and authority to overcome Satan and
evil spirits at their most profound level of activity."

How do you cast out a demon?

First, ask yourself if it is a condition of demonization you can
handle. If not, you may wish to ask one or two others to assist you, or
refer the person to someone who is competent in spiritual ministry. If
you are not sure, ask God if He is leading you to become involved.

Second, prepare yourself. Pray, asking for the anointing of power
and the discerning of spirits. Jesus taught His disciples that some evil
spirits do not respond to just anyone, anytime. Some people are deliv-

ered only after fervent prayer and fasting (Mark 9:29).

Third, ask the demonized person to prepare for ministry with prayer and fasting. This is not possible, of course, if the individual is heavily oppressed.

Fourth, minister deliverance privately whenever possible. If I am caught off guard in a public meeting by an unexpected demonic manifestation, I try to have the demonized person removed to another room. Demons seem to like attention. Furthermore, observing a deliverance can be very frightening to people who are not familiar with that kind of ministry.

Fifth, in the name of Jesus command the spirit, by name if necessary, to leave. Remember, the power of God has to do with Christ in you and the Spirit working through you, not the volume of your voice.

The Limitations of Deliverance

Deliverance is not a cure-all. Not every human problem has a demonic origin. James wrote, "When tempted, no one should say, 'God is tempting me.' For God cannot be tempted by evil, nor does he tempt anyone; but each one is tempted [not by the devil here but] by his own evil desire" (James 1:13-14). Jesus addressed this when He declared, "Out of the heart come evil thoughts, murder, adultery, sexual immorality, theft, false testimony, slander" (Matthew 15:19).

Matthew Linn writes, "Those who see a need only for deliverance err just as greatly as those who see a need only for medicine, only for psychiatric treatment, or only for environmental change when several or all of these factors may contribute to a person's suffering."[11] Demons are real. Demons influence human behavior. But never use demons as an excuse for personal sin or spiritual irresponsibility. Most human behavior is not demonic.

Deliverance does not always last. Even when a release from an evil spirit occurs, it does not guarantee permanent freedom. Deliverance must be accompanied by a commitment to obey God's Word and grow in Christ. Sometimes, if not always, personal accountability to other mature Christians is necessary during the transition period. Satan's government must be exchanged for God's, not just cast out. Jesus taught:

> When an evil spirit comes out of a man, it goes through arid places seeking rest and does not find it. Then it says, "I will return to the house I left." When it arrives, it finds the house unoccupied, swept clean and put in order. Then it goes and takes with it seven other spirits more wicked than itself, and they go in and live there. And the final condition of that man is worse than the first.
>
> MATTHEW 12:43-45

Deliverance does not always "work." I have prayed for people to be delivered from what appeared to be unmistakably demonic symptoms, and their problems have not gone away. When praying with someone, we need to know not only when to begin but when to stop. There may be other factors that require us to withdraw our forces in order to consider the problem from other angles. Sometimes there is a demon at work, sometimes not. Sometimes we lack faith.

Demonization and deliverance are not the primary subject of this book, and I have attempted to discuss a sensitive and difficult subject in a relatively short space. The elusive, deceptive nature of demons can make deliverance ministry extremely complex. For those who want more information on it, I recommend the books cited in this chapter, as well as books on deliverance by Neil Anderson.

Spiritual warfare is serious business, but keep asking God for discernment and power. If there is work to be done, He will show you how to do it.

TWELVE

All Kinds of Prayer

And pray in the Spirit on all occasions with all kinds of prayers and requests. With this in mind, be alert and always keep on praying for all the saints.

EPHESIANS 6:18

W e are living in what is perhaps the greatest prayer revival in history. Thousands of Christians and church leaders are gathering all over North America and around the world for special corporate prayer meetings.

Pray! And then pray some more! Spiritual warfare is real, and prayer has a militant purpose: to overcome the dominion of darkness in order to bring about change in people and society. The kingdom of God is at hand, and the saints of God have a great weapon in prayer. We wrestle not with flesh-and-blood human problems. "With this in mind, be alert and always keep on praying for all the saints."

Ironically, even with growing worldwide participation, prayer is something that the majority of Christians seem to neglect with a passion. At least four times a year our church devotes a full evening service to corporate prayer. Regrettably, they are our most poorly attended public meetings. I am convinced that spiritual blindness is the basic cause of prayerlessness.

The more clearly you see the spiritual realm, the more you will pray; and conversely, the more you pray, the more you will see clearly the spiritual realm. A growing awareness of spiritual warfare will always bring with it an increasing commitment to pray. The two go hand in hand. Prayer puts us in touch with the spiritual dimension and releases the power of God.

The deeply spiritual Andrew Murray wrote in *The Ministry of Intercession:*

> As one looks back on the history of the early church, how clear these two great truths stand out: 1) where there is much prayer, there will be much of the Spirit; and 2) where there is much of the Spirit, there will be ever-increasing prayer.[1]

Paul wraps up his discussion of spiritual warfare and weaponry in Ephesians 6 by making perhaps the most comprehensive and powerful declaration about prayer in all of Scripture. Here is my paraphrase of Ephesians 6:17-18:

> And all of you together, take up the helmet of salvation and the sword of the Spirit, the one that is the word [*rhema*] of God.[2] How do you do this? Through all prayer and petition, *praying constantly in every season, opportunity, or crisis* in the Spirit, for the purpose of watching constantly[3] with all perseverance and prayer concerning all the saints.

The four lessons here, though simple, are critical. *First,* prayer is incredibly important. Notice that verse 18 explains *how* to take up the helmet and sword for battle. Without prayer there is no armor. Without prayer we are spiritually naked. Prayer is a matter of spiritual life and death.

Second, prayer *in the Spirit* is incredibly important. Prayer is a spiritual exercise, and the ultimate power of prayer is not how well you pray or even how long you pray but rather the participation of the Spirit. Jude echoes Paul's words: "Build yourselves up in your most holy faith and pray *in the Holy Spirit"* (Jude 20).

We must confront the spirit power of the dominion of darkness by the Spirit power of prayer. "The weapons we fight with are not the weapons of the world. On the contrary, they have divine power to demolish strongholds" (2 Corinthians 10:4).

Third, prayer is incredibly important in every situation. We are to pray constantly, without ceasing, "on all occasions." Can you imagine Jesus' facing anything in life without first seeking the will of His Father? Everything in life, without exception, is an occasion for prayer, even if we are not dealing directly with a demon.

Fourth, all kinds of prayer are important. People often ask me, *"How* should I pray?" This question implies that prayer is a kind of spiritual formula: Get all the words right, and God is bound to answer. It is as if Christians are playing a game of heavenly battleship, calling out grid numbers to God in hopes that He will say, "Hit!"

How should I pray? I have a simple answer: Just pray! Then pray some more. Pray however you need to pray, as long as you need to pray, until you break through to God. "Pray in the Spirit on all occasions with all kinds of prayers and requests."

Elements of Prayer

The struggle, generally, is not so much in knowing how to pray but in taking time to do it. Busyness has nothing to do with how many responsibilities you have; it is your state of mind. Jesus compassionately rebuked Mary's sister, "Martha, Martha, you are worried and upset about many things, but only one thing is needed. Mary has chosen what is better, and it will not be taken away from her" (Luke 10:41-42). Mary chose to sit in the presence of Jesus.

The practice of prayer is really very simple. "All kinds of prayers" have four common elements.

First, prayer is talking with God. I am indebted to my wife, Marilyn, for this definition. Preparing a sermon series on prayer, I asked her to complete the sentence "Prayer is ..." Her immediate, simple, and perfect answer: Prayer is talking with God. You can talk to God as you would a close friend. Without being afraid, you can tell Him exactly what you are thinking and feeling—or that you are confused and don't know what to think or feel.

Second, prayer is listening to God. Prayer is not frenzied begging. Listening prayer is quieting your soul, letting God converse with you out of the Scriptures. Listening prayer is opening your heart to God, allowing Him to speak into the ear of your spirit. When you hear God's voice, your thoughts will change, and when your thoughts change, your feelings and behavior will change.

Third, prayer is asking. "You do not have, because you do not ask God" (James 4:2). When your prayer requests are specific, it says two things about what you really believe. One, it demonstrates that you really believe there is a God. Two, it demonstrates that you believe God cares enough about you personally to answer your prayer.

Does this seem too simplistic? Well, just the opposite is true: *Not* being specific in your prayers is a sign of unbelief. Generic prayers may give you a warm feeling, but they also give you and God an out. When you pray specific prayers, it puts both you and God on the spot. The risk is that God might say no. But then He might say yes!

When our children were small, they never hesitated to ask us for specific things, regardless of how outrageous their requests may have been. And rarely did they take no for an answer. As kids get older, they get wiser—and more evasive. Kids learn how to ask for things more shrewdly because they are afraid they will get the wrong answer. But you cannot help your kids if you are not sure what they are asking for.

God, of course, perceives all of our subtle intentions. He even knows our needs before we ask, but He still expects us to pray, and to pray specifically. It never hurts to ask. It may hurt when the answer is no, but being specific in prayer means that we must be open to the will of the Father, regardless of the answer.

If you pray vague prayers, you may never know what God is saying. The writer of Hebrews declared, "Without faith it is impossible to please God, because anyone who comes to him must believe that he exists and that he rewards those who earnestly seek him" (Hebrews 11:6).

Fourth, prayer is believing. There is, of course, a difference between "just praying" (something I call "bedtime prayers") and passionate prayer. "The prayer *offered in faith,*" James writes, "will make the sick person well" (5:16). The King James translation refers to this as "effectual fervent" prayer. So important is our faith that even Jesus Himself, when faced with the lack of it in those around Him, "could not do any miracles there, except lay his hands on a few sick people and heal them. And he was amazed at their lack of faith" (Mark 6:5-6).

Intercession

Intercession is one of the many "kinds of prayer." Although the Greek terms for intercession (*enteuxis* and *entugchano*) are used sparingly in the New Testament and not at all in Ephesians 6, it is an important aspect of prayer. *Precede* means "go before"; *recede* means "go back"; *intercede* means "go between."

Ezekiel voiced Jehovah's pain: "I looked for a man among them who would build up the wall and stand before me in the gap on behalf of the land so I would not have to destroy it, but I found none" (22:30). Intercessory prayer is standing in the gap, becoming an intermediary in the spiritual realm. There is only one Mediator between God and man: Jesus Christ. But we become mediators of God's kingdom when we intercede for our families, our friends, and our nation and work to break the powers of darkness over them.

Intercession is redemptive praying, carrying us beyond our own selfish needs and bearing the burdens of others. In intercessory prayer we merge with the very heart of God.

Intercession is sacrificial, fervent prayer, of which Jesus is our example: "He is able to save completely those who come to God through him, because he always lives to intercede for them" (Hebrews 7:25).

Intercession is spiritual tenacity. The intensity of our intercession, however, is not measured by how much energy we expend or how tired we are when the praying is over. The power of intercession is gauged by how persistently we pray and how sincerely we believe.

As a conclusion to the parable of the persistent friend, Jesus declared:

Ask and keep on asking, and it shall be given you; seek and keep on seeking, and you shall find; knock and keep on knocking, and the door shall be opened to you. For every one who asks and keeps on asking receives, and he who seeks and keeps on seeking finds, and to him who knocks and keeps on knocking the door shall be opened.

Luke 11:9-10, Amplified[4]

Furthermore, intercessory prayer is kingdom activity. In prayer, believers draw on the powers of the age to come. The kingdom power of prayer is unveiled in one of the most terrifying passages in the Bible, Revelation 8.

John had had an earlier vision of martyred souls crying out to God, "How long, Sovereign Lord, holy and true, until you judge the inhabitants of the earth and avenge our blood?" (6:10). Revelation 8, a chilling panorama of global judgment, is the direct outcome of this prayer:

> Another angel, who had a golden censer, came and stood at the altar. He was given much incense [the aroma of Christ's finished work] to offer, with the prayers of all the saints, on the golden altar before the throne. The smoke of the incense, together with the prayers of the saints, went up before God from the angel's hand. Then the angel took the censer, filled it with fire from the altar, *and hurled it on the earth;* and there came peals of thunder, rumblings, flashes of lightning and an earthquake.
>
> REVELATION 8:3-5

The implication here is that what happens on the earth is the direct aftermath of the prayers of the saints reaching the throne of God. Masterful writer Eugene Peterson maintains in *Earth and Altar:*

> Prayer is political action. Prayer is social energy. Prayer is public good. Far more of our nation's life is shaped by prayer than is formed by legislation. That we have not collapsed into anarchy is due more to prayer than to the police. The single most important action contributing to whatever health and strength there is in our land is prayer.
>
> We don't need a new movement to save America. The old movement is holding its own and making its way very well. We don't need a new campaign, a new consciousness-raising, a new

program, new legislation, new politics or a new reformation. The people who meet in worship and offer themselves in acts of prayer are doing what needs to be done.[5]

Prayer Changes Things

Prayer changes things. This is the not-so-obvious assumption of Paul's great challenge to pray on the battlefield of the spirit. If we wrestle with principalities and powers of darkness, then prayer is designed to accomplish something.

R.A. Torrey, influential in the founding of Biola University (California), wrote in *The Power of Prayer:*

> A very considerable proportion of the membership of our evangelical churches today do not believe even theoretically in prayer, that is, they do not believe in prayer as bringing anything to pass that would not have come to pass if they had not prayed. They believe in prayer as having a beneficial "reflex influence," that is, as benefitting the person who prays, but as for prayer bringing anything to pass that would not have come to pass if we had not prayed, they do not believe in it.[6]

Numerous scriptures teach clearly that prayer changes *things.* James calls Elijah "a man just like us." He prayed earnestly that it would not rain, and it did not—for three-and-a-half years! Then he prayed again, and it rained. The lesson: "The prayer of a righteous man is powerful and effective" (see James 5:16-18).

Even scientific inquiry has demonstrated that prayer changes things. An article in the *Journal of the American Medical Association* described measurable effects of prayer. Heart patients in a particular unit were randomly divided into two groups of approximately two hundred each. The first group received prayer by Christians; the "control group" did not. The article states, "The control patients required ventilatory assistance, antibiotics, and diuretics more frequently than patients [receiving prayer]."[7] It was a double-blind study, meaning neither doctors nor patients knew who was being prayed for. Prayer changes things!

Prayer Changes You

When you pray, you are placing yourself under the lordship of Christ. Your priorities change. You change. In fact, the obedient, disciplined life of prayer is a statement about your personal priorities. As I said earlier, a priority is not what you think is important; it is what you do with your time. Prayer changes you three ways: spiritually, mentally/emotionally, and physically.

First, prayer changes you spiritually. This is self-evident. The more time you spend in prayer, the more you will have a spiritual outlook. Jude's how-to for "[building] yourselves up in your most holy faith" was to "pray in the Holy Spirit" (verse 20). R.A. Torrey penned these words:

> Prayer will promote our personal piety, our individual holiness, our individual growth into the likeness of our Lord Jesus Christ as almost nothing else. Here is the secret of becoming much like God, remaining long with God.[8]

If life is a spiritual battle, then we need spiritual power. Prayer makes us strong in the character of God and in the authority of Christ. Prayerlessness, on the other hand, increases our spiritual vulnerability.

Second, prayer changes you mentally and emotionally. Personal change is grounded in spiritual change. When you change spiritually by deepening your reliance on God, you change mentally and emotionally. To repeat a key spiritual warfare scripture, "The weapons we fight with have divine power to demolish strongholds," which include imaginations, arguments, pretensions—every thought that "sets itself up against the knowledge of God" (see 2 Corinthians 10:3-5).

Prayer brings us under the government of God, and where God rules there is peace. Isaiah put it this way: "Of the increase of his government *and peace* there will be no end" (9:7). And in another place and on a more personal level, the same prophet said, "You will keep in perfect peace him whose mind is steadfast, because he trusts in you" (26:3).

In an earlier chapter I described a time of personal trauma. Spiritual warfare, coupled with God's demand for change in me and my own emotional upheaval, drove me to prayer and fasting. On one occasion, under the supervision and spiritual care of a Christian friend and counselor, I fasted for three days for release and emotional healing. Fasting is perhaps the most fervent way of praying.

During my fast, my wife's cousin visited us. A physician, he is not a professing Christian. Naturally, he was curious as to why I was refraining from a particularly delicious meal Marilyn had prepared. I thought for a moment. How was I going to explain fasting and spiritual warfare? And then it hit me: I was fasting, I told him, because I was going through a difficult time, and fasting is a personal discipline that helps me get on top of my emotions.

Others have told me the same thing: "The only way I can control my emotions is by fasting." Concentrated prayer and fasting can have a dramatically calming effect on emotions, and emotional stability is a key to victory in spiritual warfare. In contrast, emotional instability—anger, self-pity, fear—may become an open door to spiritual oppression.

Nothing—not counseling, teaching cassettes, Christian television—*nothing* can substitute for fervent personal prayer. Jesus said, "This kind [of demon] does not go out except by prayer and fasting" (Matthew 17:21).[9]

Third, prayer changes you physically. Listen to the wonderful, familiar prophecy of Isaiah 40:

> The Lord is the everlasting God....
> He gives strength to the weary
>   and increases the power of the weak.
> Even youths grow tired and weary,
> And young men stumble and fall;
>   but those who hope in the Lord
>   will renew their strength.
> They will soar on wings like eagles;
>   they will run and not grow weary,
>   they will walk and not be faint.
>
> ISAIAH 40:28-30

Prayer for Physical Healing

How does prayer for physical healing work?

First, it releases the power of God. God works directly through prayer. It was the power of God in the ministry of Jesus that healed the sick. Several times the sicknesses that Jesus healed were associated with spirits of infirmity (Luke 13:10-17, for example), which points out even more clearly the need for spiritual power through prayer.

Second, prayer brings healing and health because it is the prototype of positive thinking. Dr. Art Mollen wrote in his syndicated newspaper column:

> People weather emergencies in different ways. A few, unprepared for adversity, react angrily, looking to blame others. Such people lack spiritual health. They accumulate resentment with life's setbacks and may suffer from ulcers, heart attacks and cancer. Others grow from tragedies. They have the spiritual shoring up to handle difficulties and may even be healthier....
>
> "Prayer is essentially a form of meditation that induces relaxation, including a decrease in the response of our nervous system," Dr. Herbert Benson writes in *Beyond the Relaxation Response: Harnessing the Healing Power of Your Personal Beliefs.*
>
> Regular prayer, like regular exercise, works best, he notes. It can improve digestive problems and insomnia; it can lower blood pressure, reducing tension headaches, irritability and fatigue; it may even prevent heart attacks.

Benson is not to my knowledge a professing Christian and is referring here only to the physiological benefits of prayer. Molen and Benson and others have merely rediscovered what the Bible has promised for thousands of years: "The prayer offered in faith will make the sick person well" (James 5:15). Scripture clearly affirms the relationship between spiritual well-being and physical health: "Do not be wise in your own eyes; fear the Lord and shun evil. This will bring health to your body and nourishment to your bones" (Proverbs 3:7-8). God's words of wisdom "are life to those who find them and health to a man's whole body" (Proverbs 4:22).

Prayer is talking, listening, asking, believing. Prayer is powerful. Prayer changes things. Prayer changes us spiritually, emotionally, and physically. Prayer is our source of strength and guidance in spiritual warfare. Therefore, "pray in the Spirit on all occasions with all kinds of prayer and requests. With this in mind, be alert and always keep on praying for all the saints."

Knowing how to pray is easy; doing it is a spiritual battle in itself. Pray. Pray often. Pray now:

Heavenly Father, teach me to pray. I realize that my problem is not ignorance but disobedience. Forgive me for my prayerlessness. Open my eyes to the spiritual realm so I will realize how necessary prayer is every day of my life.

Help me to pray. Renew and deepen my prayer life. In the name of Jesus, who taught us to pray, Amen.

THIRTEEN

Confronting the Difficulties of Prayer

We do not know what we ought to pray, but the Spirit himself inter-cedes for us with groans that words cannot express.

ROMANS 8:26

As the title of Dick Eastman's classic book on prayer proclaims, it is "no easy road." It is hard enough to establish a habit of prayer. But when you do and nothing happens to reward you for your effort, devastating discouragement may creep in. You may even begin resenting God.

When you have prayed every way you know how, then what? Is Satan resisting you? Is he winning? Are you missing something? Have you forgotten to put on a piece of the armor?

The Frustration of Not Knowing How to Pray

Prayer is not a bag of spiritual tricks. Prayer reduced to a formula is not prayer. After reading every book on the subject, after experimenting with every technique and exploring every prayer "secret," sometime, sooner or later, inevitably, you will come to a sense of helplessness and frustration.

What then? Read just one more book? Memorize one more scripture? Get just a little more faith? Like Job's counselors, our well-meaning

Christian friends will keep trying to help us discover the "ultimate cause" of our problem.

What we have to realize is that some situations defy ultimate explanations. The apostle Paul wrote, "We know in part and we prophesy in part" (1 Corinthians 13:9). When we have done our very best, we are still weak warriors. In this present age, no matter how spiritually sensitive and wise we become, this is the reality: "We are looking in a mirror that gives only a dim (blurred) reflection [of reality as in a riddle or enigma]" (1 Corinthians 12:12, AMPLIFIED). We pray in part, and sometimes we do not know how to pray at all.

A member of my church handed me this little story from the business publication *Bits and Pieces:*

An elderly gentleman passed his granddaughter's room one night and overheard her repeating the alphabet in an oddly reverent way. "What on earth are you up to?" he asked.

"I'm saying my prayers," explained the little girl. "But I can't think of exactly the right words tonight, so I'm just saying all the letters. God will put them together for me, because he knows what I'm thinking."[1]

This reminded me of Jesus' pronouncement, "I am the Alpha and the Omega,[2] the Beginning and the End" (Revelation 21:6). Jesus is everything in the middle, too. He is God's encyclopedia of answers for human problems. When all that we can muster is a garbled prayer, God puts the sounds and letters together.

God Helps Those Who *Can't* Help Themselves

"In the same way, the Spirit helps us in our weakness. We do not know what we ought to pray, but the Spirit himself intercedes for us with groans that words cannot express" (Romans 8:26). The King James reads, "For we know not what we should pray for as we ought," suggesting two of the most frustrating aspects of prayer: not knowing what to pray and not knowing how. *The Amplified Bible* points this out as well: "For we do not know what prayer to offer *nor* how to offer it worthily as we ought."

This verse about the Spirit's intercession is in the middle of what is widely considered one of the most important chapters in the Bible, Romans 8. A few highlights from this chapter, then, are important for understanding verse 26.

First, life can be a real mess. Paul writes:

The creation waits in eager expectation for the sons of God to be revealed. For the creation was subjected to frustration, not by its own choice, but by the will of the one who subjected it, in hope that the creation itself will be liberated from its bondage to decay and brought into the glorious freedom of the children of God.

We know that the whole creation has been groaning as in the pains of childbirth right up to the present time. Not only so, but we ourselves, who have the first fruits of the Spirit, groan inwardly as we wait eagerly for our adoption as sons, the redemption of our bodies.

ROMANS 8:19-23

Simply stated, life is not what it ought to be, nor is it what it will be. Life is difficult at best, and we are all groaning for a better world. The whole world groans.[3]

I was asked to preside at a funeral for a family I did not know. It was as sad a service as I have ever seen. A mother and her twenty-four-year-old invalid daughter were in a serious car accident that killed the mother. At the close of the service, a family member rolled the daughter's wheelchair to the side of the coffin.

I wasn't sure she could understand what was happening—until she broke into the most pathetic weeping I have ever heard. I cried. Everyone cried. The woman in the coffin had spent all her waking hours lovingly caring for a human being who would now probably have to be institutionalized.

What do you say in a situation like that? What do you pray? It is no wonder that Paul declared, "I consider that our present sufferings are not worth comparing with the glory that will be revealed in us." Paul is idealistic in the proper sense, but he is also realistic. Life is so difficult at times, the warfare so intense, that "we know not what we should pray for as we ought." We don't know what to say. We don't know what to pray. We don't know how to pray.

The only hope for a groaning cosmos, according to Romans 8, is God's threefold provision: first, the certainty of the resurrection and ultimate renewal of the entire universe (verses 20-23); second, the promise that somehow everything will work together for good for those who love God (verse 28); and third, the constant intercession of the Holy Spirit (verse 27). When we don't know how to pray or what to pray or can't pray, the Spirit intercedes on our behalf with a groaning of empathy and power that overcomes the groanings of a dark world.[4]

What does this have to do with spiritual warfare? Paul's conclusion in Romans 8:34-39 is clear:

Christ Jesus is at the right of God *and is also interceding for us.* Who [then] shall separate us from the love of Christ? I am convinced that neither death nor life, neither angels *nor demons,* neither the present nor the future, nor any powers [social, political, *or spiritual*], neither height nor depth, nor anything else in all creation, will be able to separate us from the love of God that is in Christ Jesus our Lord.

Fear Not

When you feel the dominion of darkness closing in on you, and it seems you are losing the battle, *fear not!* Jesus is praying for you. Two powerful passages in the Bible, one in the Old Testament and one in the New, illustrate the effectual intercessory work of Christ in the spiritual battle for your soul.

The first is Zechariah 3, where "Joshua the high priest [is] standing before the angel of the Lord, and Satan [is] standing at his right side to accuse him" (verse 1). In the historical setting of this text, many Israelites were returning from Babylonian exile to rebuild the city of Jerusalem and the temple of Jehovah, leveled in a siege some seventy years earlier. Joshua, the current high priest of the new Israel,[5] represented the high point of spirituality, the cream of the Jewish nation. But his religious best was not good enough, because "Joshua was dressed in filthy clothes as he stood before the angel" (verse 3). Satan really had the right to accuse him!

When I look at my life, even the best days of my walk with God, I know that it is impossible to avoid some kind of attitude or thought that would give Satan cause to accuse me. So when the answers to my prayers are delayed, my failures—sometimes the littlest ones—stare me in the face. It is precisely these failures that Satan targets with his vicious accusations and killer condemnation.

We try desperately to close every door to spiritual oppression, but Satan knows what's in our closets. Self-cleansing is spiritually self-defeating. Our only certain defense against the dominion of darkness is the angel of the Lord, Jesus Christ, interceding for us as He did for Joshua. "The Lord said to Satan, 'The Lord rebuke you, Satan! The Lord, who has chosen Jerusalem, rebuke you!'" (verse 2). Romans 8:33 echoes, "Who will bring any charge against those whom God has chosen?"

Next, the angel of the Lord deals with Joshua's sins:

> [He] said to those who were standing before him, "Take off his filthy clothes." Then he said to Joshua, "See, I have taken away your sin, and I will put rich garments on you." Then [he] said, "Put a clean turban on his head." So they put a clean turban on his head and clothed him, while the angel of the Lord stood by.
>
> Zechariah 3:4-5

All of this prefigures the work of Christ in the New Testament. He exchanges the filthy rags of our own works (Isaiah 64:6) for the glistening, spotless robe of His righteousness (Revelation 19:7-8). "Therefore he is able to save *completely* those who come to God through him, *because he always lives to intercede for them*" (Hebrews 7:25).

The story of Peter's triple denial is an equally dramatic illustration of the power of Christ's intercession for us in the battle for our souls. Before His crucifixion, Jesus pierced Peter's heart with a painful prophecy: "Simon, Simon, Satan has asked to sift you as wheat. *But I have prayed for you*, Simon, that your faith may not fail. And when you have turned back, strengthen your brothers" (Luke 22:31-32).

From my point of view there are times when my faith, like Peter's, seems to fail. It looks as though Satan has won and I have become the victim of his schemes. But this story of Peter and Jesus' prayers for him offers comfort. When my relationship with God seems to have taken a nosedive, Jesus is still praying that my faith will not fail. The incense of Christ's sacrifice on Calvary is mingled with my feeble prayers, so that by the time they reach the throne of God, all my words and letters, like the little girl's in the story, have been rearranged (see Revelation 8:1-4).

Jesus even commanded Peter to strengthen his brothers after the ordeal of his denial! How could Peter strengthen anyone? He was a failure. He willfully and maliciously denied Jesus three times. But Peter learned an unforgettable lesson in grace. His testimony to his brothers was that, while his *own* strength failed, the intercessory prayer of Jesus shielded his soul from satanic penetration.

I am a conqueror in spiritual warfare, ultimately, not because *my* faith endures but because Jesus prays for my faith to endure. When you don't know what to pray or how to pray, or when you don't even feel like praying, the Holy Spirit is interceding for you with inexpressible groanings. And so is Jesus. If God be for us, who in heaven, earth, or hell can stand against us! "We are more than conquerors *through him*" (Romans 8:37). "Thanks be to God, who *always* leads us in triumphal procession in Christ" (2 Corinthians 2:14).

The Guilt of Unanswered Prayer

If I have done everything I know to do, and Jesus is praying for me, then why are some prayers never answered? Just today a woman in our church called for comfort and to ask if I would conduct her husband's funeral. A Christian, this man had been seriously injured in a 1980 car wreck in which he was intoxicated. His life since the accident had been a roller coaster of seizures and more drinking. It was a seizure that killed him.

His wife has been praying for years. He prayed, too—when he was not overwhelmed by guilt for his sinful life. Prayer is supposed to change things. Did their prayers fail? Did Jesus' prayers fail? Did Satan win?

Prayer, faith, healing ministry, resisting the devil and his dominion of darkness, all are related concepts. And all things being equal, when they don't "work," it raises perhaps the most difficult issues of the Christian life. At the root is the age-old question, Why do bad things happen to good people? If we are "good," why do our prayers of faith remain unanswered? Why does evil seem to win? I don't have all the answers, but I have some ideas that have helped me.

An essential principle of Christianity is that faith works. That's why we pray. Resist the devil and he will flee from you, for greater is Jesus in you than the devil in the world. I diagram it this way:

Faith   ——————▶   Results

Faith produces results. This is simple logic, supported by numerous Bible verses. Hebrews 11:6 is particularly clear on this point: "Without faith it is impossible to please God, because anyone who comes to him must believe that he exists and that he rewards those who earnestly seek him."

But here is where the simple logic breaks down. We know this is true:

Faith   ——————▶   Results

We assume, then, that this is also true:

No Faith   ——————▶   No Results

No results, we think, is a sure sign that there is no faith, or at least not enough faith or not enough prayer or not enough spiritual power. The effect of this is discouragement or alarm or a sense of failure and defeat, or even a waning trust in God.

There Must Be Something Wrong With Me

A young couple in our church were expecting their third child. Everything pointed to a normal pregnancy, but the mother-to-be went into sudden labor a couple of months before the baby was due. She was rushed to the hospital and gave birth to a little boy with severe genetic deformities.

I was the first one they called. They were so distraught they wanted pastoral counsel and ministry before asking their family to visit the child. I will never forget the very first thing this young, suffering mother asked me: "Do you think something wrong in me allowed this to happen?"

"No," I responded with firm conviction, remembering the man born blind and Jesus' words that sin in his parents was not the reason (see John 9). "This is difficult enough without your having to suffer a sense of condemnation too!" She was actually thinking that her horrible personal crisis was caused by some moral or spiritual lack on her part. "No results," or in this case bad results, was interpreted by this couple as a lack of faith.

Hebrews 11 is probably the most lengthy and thorough treatment of overcoming faith in the Bible. After the well-known definition of faith in verse 1, "Faith is the evidence of things not seen," the writer explains how faith worked in the lives of famous Old Testament heroes. As we might expect, most of the examples in the chapter demonstrate that faith produces results: *"Through faith* [they] conquered kingdoms, administered justice, and gained what was promised"* (verse 33).

But notice the change in the middle of verse 35: The list of "successful" saints ends with the first half of the verse: "Women received back their dead, raised to life again." Almost imperceptibly the ballad changes to a minor key: *"Others* were tortured and refused to be released.... They were stoned; they were sawed in two; they were put to death by the sword. They went about in sheepskins and goatskins, destitute, persecuted and mistreated."

Did the dominion of darkness win? Was something wrong with their faith? No! In fact, these "were all commended for their faith, yet none of them received what had been promised" (verse 39).

Faith, then, is not measured by tangible results alone. Sometimes it is measured by perseverance, even when there are no visible results! Earlier in Hebrews 11 we find these words about those we consider "successful" in their faith: "All these people were still living by faith when they died. They did not receive the things promised; they only saw them and welcomed them from a distance" (verse 13).

Facing Failure Realistically

Matthew 13 is a unique explanation of this contradiction. In this chapter Jesus presents the parables of the kingdom. Remember that spiritual warfare is a clash of the kingdoms. Surprisingly, these parables do not seem to be about the wonderful success of God's kingdom but of its impurities and apparent failures: seeds that seem to be wasted (verses 3-23); yeast in the dough (verse 33); a net that catches "all kinds of fish," good and bad (verses 47-50).

In other words, Jesus is teaching His disciples how to face *failure in the kingdom* realistically. The parable of the wheat and the weeds (verses 24-30, 37-43) illustrates this most profoundly: "The kingdom of heaven is like a man who sowed good seed in his field. But while everyone was sleeping, his enemy came and sowed weeds among the wheat."

Jesus explained, "The one who sowed the good seed is the Son of Man. The field is the world, and the good seed stands for the sons of the kingdom. The weeds are *the sons of the evil one,* and the enemy who sows them *is the devil.*"

The servants ask the owner of the field, "Do you want us to go and pull the weeds up?"

"No," he answers, "because while you are pulling the weeds, you may root up the wheat with them. Let them both grow together until the harvest."

Let them both grow together? How could Jesus say this?

It is an important lesson: We have to learn to live with the possibility of failure, even in spiritual warfare. Now, this does not mean that we give up! Winning in life is walking with God—not just when the problems go away but even when it looks as if we are not winning. Paul put it this way: "I know what it is to be in need, and I know what it is to have plenty. I have learned the secret of being content in any and every situation, whether well fed or hungry, whether living in plenty or in want" (Philippians 4:12).

Thus, aggressive spiritual warfare—casting out demons, pulling down strongholds—is not the only way to overcome the dominion of darkness. Satan is foiled when we insist on praising God, even when we are engulfed in suffering.

Though the fig tree does not bud and there are no grapes on the vines, though the olive crop fails and the fields produce no food, though there are no sheep in the pen and no cattle in the stalls, yet I will rejoice in the Lord, I will be joyful in God my Savior.

HABAKKUK 3:17-18

Persistent faith in the face of adversity is a great victory. "Even in darkness light dawns for the upright. His heart is secure, he will have no fear; *in the end* he will look in triumph on his foes" (Psalm 112:4, 8).

Job stood his ground, even though Satan brought him to the brink of destruction. Much like the Book of Job, Ecclesiastes is a book of unanswered questions about the inconsistencies of life. It begins, "Meaningless! Meaningless! Utterly meaningless! Everything is meaningless" (Ecclesiastes 1:2). And yet the writer, Solomon, looking straight into the eye of life's injustice, commands, "Fear God and keep his commandments, for this is the whole duty of man" (12:13).

You can be victorious in warfare if you are willing to persevere when things look the darkest. Prayer strengthens you in the battle and brings the towers of the enemy toppling down, whether you can see it or not. As Jesus told His disciples, we "should *always pray and not give up*" (Luke 18:1).

We will win in the end.

FOURTEEN

The Kingdom Power of Praise

May the praise of God be in their mouths and a double-edged sword in their hands, to inflict vengeance on the nations and punishment on the peoples, to bind their kings with fetters, their nobles with shackles of iron, to carry out the sentence written against them.

PSALM 149:6-9

Worship is the ultimate weapon in spiritual conflict. Whoever or whatever gets worshiped, directly or indirectly, becomes the higher authority of the one worshiping. And wherever there is acknowledgment of a higher authority, there is control and dominion—a kingdom.

Praise is kingdom activity. Praise of Jesus is an aggressive affirmation before the audiences of heaven, earth, and hell that He is Lord! It is both the confession of your mouth (speaking, singing) that Jesus is Lord *and* a lifestyle of obedience and service to Him.

Over against true worship, Satan's ageless obsession has been to depose God and redirect the adoration of the universe to himself. In what is widely believed to be a reference to the downfall of Satan, Isaiah wrote:

How you have fallen from heaven, O morning star [*Lucifer* in the KJV], son of the dawn! You who once laid low the nations! You said in your heart, "I will ascend to heaven; I will raise my throne above the stars of God; I will sit enthroned on the mount of assembly, on the utmost heights of the sacred mountain. I will make myself like the Most High."

ISAIAH 14:12-14

When Jesus came to reestablish God's kingdom in the earth, Satan shrewdly offered Him a shortcut to victory, an easy way out of the cross. He proposed to give Jesus authority over all the kingdoms of this world in exchange for a few moments of worship. Satan knew that an instant of praise from the Son of God would have had devastating consequences.

Whom *you* praise and what *you* worship have enormous implications, because whomever or whatever you worship will become the master of your soul. Listen to the frightful conditions of the last days: "The whole world was astonished and followed the beast [the Antichrist]. *Men worshiped the dragon* because he had given authority to the beast, *and they also worshiped the beast"* (Revelation 13:3-4).

The terrible result: The beast gained absolute control over their lives. A second beast, a kind of unholy spirit, gives life to the son of Satan:

He was given power to give breath to the image of the first beast, so that it could speak and cause all who refused to worship the image to be killed. He also forced everyone, small and great, rich and poor, free and slave, to receive a mark on his right hand or on his forehead, so that no one could buy or sell unless he had the mark.

REVELATION 13:15-17

Worship is not just the songs you sing. It is the submission of your life to a higher power. Jesus says it very simply: "No one can serve two masters. Either he will hate the one and love the other, or he will be devoted to the one and despise the other. You cannot serve both God and Money" (Matthew 6:24). Every person *will* worship. Devotion to something or someone is an essential element of human life.

The Greek term Jesus uses for "money" is *mamonas*, or "mammon." Kittel's *Theological Dictionary of the New Testament* indicates on page 55 that this word seems to have come from an Aramaic[1] root that means "that in which one trusts." So whatever you worship you will trust. The object of your worship will become the focus of your faith—like your career, or a particular relationship, or money, or possessions. Maybe even yourself. And what you worship will rule your life.

Praise and God's Presence

How important are praise and worship to God? In Psalm 87 we discover that the Lord loves the gates of Zion more than all the dwellings of Jacob (verse 2). All the dwellings *of Jacob?* We might expect the psalmist to write that God loves the gates of Zion more than all the dwellings of Egypt or Assyria. But instead, he compares God's feelings about Zion, or Jerusalem, with the other cities and villages of Jacob, that is, Israel.

What does that mean? That God favors Zion over the other dwellings of Israel? Isn't He omnipresent? Why would He prefer one place to another?

The Bible teaches that God is particular about where He reveals His *special* presence, something the Jews called the *shekinah*. The *shekinah* could be found in only one place: above the Ark of the Covenant in the Holy of Holies, in the tabernacle and later in the temple. In conjunction with this, God's special *shekinah* presence became associated with the capital city and spiritual stronghold of the nation of Israel.

Psalm 87 tells us specifically that God loves *the gates* of Zion more than all the dwellings of Jacob. What is it about those gates that attracts God's attention? Isaiah 60, a prophecy about the future glory of Zion, opens with the proclamation, "Arise, shine [Zion], for your light has come, and the glory of the Lord [His special presence] rises upon you" (verse 1).

Later in the chapter Zion's gates are clearly identified: "You will call your walls Salvation *and your gates Praise*" (verse 18). Praise is the gateway into the presence of God. In another place the psalmist declares, "Shout for joy to the Lord, all the earth. Serve the Lord with gladness; come before him with joyful songs.... *Enter his gates with thanksgiving and his courts with praise*" (Psalm 100:1-2, 4).

Praise is also God's dwelling place: "But thou art holy, O thou that inhabitest the praises of Israel" (Psalm 22:3, KJV). Another translation reads, "Yet thou art holy, O Thou who art enthroned upon the praises of Israel" (NAS).

This points us toward the New Testament. In the Gospel of John we read that a Samaritan woman queried Jesus about the proper place to worship. To put it another way, she was asking the Messiah, "Where is God's special dwelling place, because that's where I want to worship?"

Jesus surprised her by abandoning the age-old idea that worship had to be restricted to a particular mountain or high place. Instead, He predicted, "A time is coming and has now come when the true worshipers will worship the Father in spirit and truth, for they are the kind of worshipers the Father seeks" (John 4:23).

In other words, Mount Zion is a spiritual place, not merely a geographical location. Now the literal dwelling place of God is worship—in spirit and in truth (see also 1 Peter 2:4-6). When we worship, the presence and power of God shows up to fill us with His grace and power and to scatter our spiritual enemies.

To take this a step further, the *shekinah* in the Old Testament can be associated with the coming of the Spirit in the New. The *shekinah* is the presence and power of the Holy Spirit, and where you have the presence of the Holy Spirit, you have God's power and kingdom. Over a period of forty days after His resurrection, Jesus spoke with His disciples about the kingdom of God (Acts 1:3). During this time and out of these discussions He promised, "You will receive power [kingdom authorization] when the Holy Spirit comes on you" (Acts 1:8).

A few days later, in fulfillment of Jesus' prediction, the Spirit fell on the disciples. A significant outcome was powerful, spontaneous worship: "We hear them declaring the wonders of God in our own tongues!" (Acts 2:11).

The dwelling place of God's special presence in the New Testament is His worshiping church. Pentecost was and is the outpouring of God's special presence to empower Christians to do the work of the kingdom. It's also the rich experience of spiritual worship. When the Spirit comes in power, people worship, and when people worship, the Spirit comes in power.

The Weapon of Praise

Worship is humanity's highest calling. Oh, the majesty and mystery! How can it be that human worship is the throne and dwelling place of the almighty God?! This means, too, that worship is a powerful weapon in spiritual warfare that dethrones the devil. "From the lips of children and infants you have ordained praise because of your enemies, *to silence the foe and the avenger"* (Psalm 8:2).

We have already seen that praise is the gateway to God's special presence. In the Bible, gates are also symbolic of authority and power. In an earlier chapter I discussed how *the gates of Hades* in Matthew 16:18 refers to the counsels or schemes of demonic authority. Gates, then, represent a place of control. I refer again to Kittel's authoritative *Dictionary of New Testament Theology:*

> The most likely meaning is that the gates of Hades stand for the ungodly forces of the underworld which attack the rock but cannot prevail against it. Later the "gates of Hades" figure especially in references to Christ's descent into Hades, *over whose gates he has supreme power* (pp. 974-75, italics added).

Indeed, with eyes of fire the resurrected Christ decrees, "I am the Living One; I was dead, and behold I am alive for ever and ever! And I hold the keys of death and Hades" (Revelation 1:18). It is in this context that Psalm 127:5 takes on special meaning: "Blessed is the man whose quiver is full of [children]. They will not be put to shame when they contend with their enemies *in the gate."* Gates are not only symbolic of authority; they represent the place where that authority is challenged.

Perhaps nothing teaches the power of praise more clearly than Psalm 149. The whole thrust of this psalm is the primacy and power of praise and worship, but it ends with one of the most extraordinary statements in the Bible:

May the praise of God be in their mouths and a double-edged sword in their hands, to inflict vengeance on the nations and punishment on the peoples, to bind their kings with fetters, their nobles with shackles of iron, to carry out the sentence written against them. This is the glory of all his saints.

PSALM 149:6-9

When used in conjunction with the double-edged sword of the Word (compare Hebrews 4:12), praise is a weapon. By worship and the Word we overcome the dominion of darkness, which holds the nations in its oppressive grip. By worshiping, we actually participate in God's judgment over the earth, "to carry out the sentence written against them. This is the glory of all his saints."

The Hebrew term translated "glory" is *hadar*, which means "ornament" or "splendor." According to R. Laird Harris in the *Theological Wordbook of the Old Testament*, this word is associated, among other things, with the glory of nature and man as they reflect the glory and goodness of God. When we use praise as a weapon to bind Satan's power in the earth, we are fulfilling God's purpose for creating humans: to have dominion.

This same Hebrew word is used in Psalm 8: "What is man that you are mindful of him? You crowned him with glory and honor [*hadar*]. *You made him ruler over the works of your hands; you put everything under his feet*" (verses 4-6). It is the great honor of the saints to represent God in the earth by exercising authority over the dominion of darkness.

Psalm 47 is another passage that demonstrates the relationship between praise and spiritual authority: "Clap your hands, all you nations; shout to God with cries of joy.... He subdued nations *under us*, peoples under our feet" (verses 1, 3). Praise and worship are the alternating links in the chain that binds Satan and the forces of hell. *Praise is kingdom activity.*

If you are in a spiritual battle, read the incredible story of warfare and victory in 2 Chronicles 20. Notice especially the importance of praise and worship in verses 18-22. Then pray and affirm one or more of the following triumphant kingdom psalms: 2, 46, 47, 100, 110. Speak these psalms aloud as a confession to build your faith. Speak them aloud to the audience of heaven, earth, and hell. Do it daily, or even several times a day, if your situation demands it.

> Sing praises to God, sing praises;
> Sing praises to our King, sing praises.
> For God is the King of all the earth;
> Sing to him a psalm of praise.
> God reigns over the nations;
> God is seated on his holy throne.
>
> PSALM 47:6-8

Praise and the Coming Kingdom

Old Testament prophecy even suggests that the establishment of the messianic kingdom will be uniquely characterized by praise and worship. When the kingdom is fully established, the ultimate issue of the universe, worship—the thing the devil wants to secure for himself—will be settled forever. Psalm 102 points forward to a messianic kingdom headquartered in the heavenly Jerusalem: "You will arise and have compassion on Zion, for it is time to show favor to her; the appointed time has come" (verse 13).

At this time, "the nations will fear the name of the Lord, all the kings of the earth will revere your glory.... So the name of the Lord will be declared in Zion and his praise in Jerusalem when the people and the kingdoms assemble *to worship the Lord"* (verses 15, 21-22).

This prophecy has a twofold significance. First, it refers to the gospel of the kingdom that will be preached to all nations. No longer will Jehovah's influence be limited to little Israel, but the fame of His name will cover the earth as the waters cover the sea. This happens when we obey the Great Commission to disciple the nations.

Second, the prophecy of Psalm 102 points toward the ultimate and total triumph of Christ over the nations, when the reign and rule of God will be established in a new heaven and a new earth. All the earth will bow down in unrestrained worship to God, and the kingdom of God will be established forever.

No longer will there be two masters. Satan will be thrown into the lake of fire forever. Paul puts it this way: "Therefore God exalted [Jesus] to the highest place and gave him the name that is above every name, that at the name of Jesus every knee should bow, in heaven and on earth and under the earth" (Philippians 2:9-10).

Until the Grand Ending, however, the kingdom is among us and at hand. As Ron Ford has written, "We are living in *the presence ... of the future....* The Kingdom of God *is* where the rule and reign of God is exercised and made visible."[2] And the reign of God is made visible where people worship in word and deed.

Worship is the ultimate issue of the universe. Worship is perhaps the most powerful and liberating weapon in spiritual warfare. Worship affirms the lordship of Jesus Christ over all creation and casts down the dominion of darkness.

Worship Him! Worship Him now! Release the presence, peace, and power of God into your life as you lift up the name of Jesus in adoration and praise.

Notes

Chapter 1
A Reality Check

1. Charles Kraft, "Shifting Worldviews, Sifting Attitudes," *Equipping the Saints* (September/October, 1987), 10, a publication of the Vineyard Churches.
2. Philip Jenkins, *The Next Christendom: The Coming of Global Christianity* (New York: Oxford University Press, 2002), 123.
3. Philip Jenkins, "The Next Christianity," *The Atlantic Monthly* (October 2002), 54, 129.
4. Clinton Arnold, *Powers of Darkness: Principalities and Powers in Paul's Letters* (Downers Grove, Ill.:InterVarsity, 1992), 182.

Chapter 3
The Belt of Truth

1. W. Robertson Nicoll, ed., *Expositor's Greek Testament* (New York: Doran), Vol. 3, 396.
2. M. Scott Peck, *People of the Lie: The Hope for Healing Human Evil* (Carmichael, Calif.: Touchstone Books, 1997), 207.
3. Peck, 181.
4. Kurt E. Koch, *Christian Counseling and Occultism* (Grand Rapids, Mich.: Kregel, 1980), 312.

Chapter 4
The Breastplate of Righteousness

1. Merrill F. Unger, *Demons in the World Today* (Carol Stream, Ill.: Tyndale, 1995), 116.
2. John Powell, *Why Am I Afraid to Tell You Who I Am?* (Allen, Tex.: Thomas More, 1995), 38-39.

Chapter 5
The Readiness of Peace

1. Gleason L. Archer, Bruce Waltke, and Robert Laird Harris, *Theological Wordbook of the Old Testament* (Chicago: Moody, 1980), Vol. II, 930-31.
2. Archer, Waltke, and Harris, 931.
3. Millard Erickson, *Christian Theology* (Grand Rapids, Mich.: Baker, 1998), Vol. 1, 329.
4. Walter Brueggemann, *Genesis: A Bible Commentary for Teaching and Preaching* (Louisville, Tenn.: Knox, 1986), 34.
5. Otto Weber, *Foundations of Dogmatics* (Grand Rapids, Mich.: Eerdmans, 1982), Vol. 1, 574.
6. Psalm 110, incidentally, is cited in the New Testament more often than any other Old Testament passage. See, for example, Acts 2:33-35.

Chapter 7
The Helmet of Salvation

1. Koch, *Christian Counseling and Occultism* 203.
2. C. Fred Dickason, *Demon Possession and the Christian: A New Perspective* (Wheaton, Ill.: Crossway, 1999).
3. A strong case can be made that *heart* and *mind* are used interchangeably in the Bible. In our language we distinguish between thoughts of the mind and feelings of the heart. This distinction is by no means clear in early Hebrew and later New Testament thought. An example is Proverbs 23:7: "For as he thinketh in his heart, so is he" (KJV).

Chapter 9
The Power of the Spirit

1. Michael Green, *I Believe in the Holy Spirit* (Grand Rapids, Mich.: Eerdmans, 1989), 38.

Chapter 10
Binding and Loosing

1. *The Expositor's Greek Testament*, Vol. 1, 225.
2. The Greek terms *deo* and *luo* are translations of the Hebrew *asar* and *hittir*. See Colin Brown, ed., *New International Dictionary of New Testament Theology* (Grand Rapids, Mich.: Zondervan, 1986), Vol. 2, 732.
3. Brown, Vol. 2, 733.

4. *Will be bound* and *will be loosed* are translations of the future perfect indicative.

5. Archibald Robertson, *Word Pictures in the New Testament* (Nashville: Baptist Sunday School Board, 1982), Vol. 1, 134.

Chapter 11
Demonization and Deliverance

1. Dickason, 33.

2. Matthew and Dennis Linn, eds., *Deliverance Prayer: Experiential, Psychological and Theological Approaches* (Mahwah, N.J.: Paulist, 1981), 5, 7.

3. Other references to deliverance in Jesus' ministry: Matthew 8:28-34; 9:32-34; 12:22-29, 43-45; Mark 1:21-34, 39; 3:20-29; 5:1-20; 7:24-30; 9:14-29; Luke 4:31-36, 40-41; 8:26-38; 9:37-45; 10:17-20; 11:14-26; 13:10-17.

4. Dickason, 40.

5. Kurt E. Koch, *Occult Bondage and Deliverance* (Grand Rapids, Mich.: Kregel, 1972).

6. Michael Scanlan and Randall J. Cirner, *Deliverance from Evil Spirits* (Ann Arbor, Mich.: Servant, 1980), 27-35.

7. I have avoided using the term *possession* because a Christian is "possessed" or owned by Christ alone. There is a point, however, at which a Christian's will may be ensnared by demon power. Thus, *demonization* is a term commonly used to describe demon influence beyond harassment.

8. Jessie Penn-Lewis, *War on the Saints* (Pittsburgh: Whitaker, 1996), 69.

9. Dickason, 186.

10. Scanlan and Cirner, 63.
11. Linn and Linn, 7.

Chapter 12
All Kinds of Prayer

1. Andrew Murray, *The Ministry of Intercession* (Pittsburgh: Whitaker, 2001), 28.
2. Or "the sword of the Spirit, which is what God has spoken" (EMPHASIZED).
3. The Greek term here means "sleeplessness."
4. *The Amplified Bible* reflects the linear action of the Greek verbs used in these verses.
5. Eugene H. Peterson, *Earth and Altar: The Community of Prayer in a Selfbound Society* (Downers Grove, Ill.: Intervarsity, 1985), 15, 21.
6. R.A. Torrey, *The Power of Prayer* (Pittsburgh: Whitaker, 2000), 15.
7. "Positive Therapeutic Effects of Intercessory Prayer in a Coronary Unit Population," *Journal of the American Medical Association* (January 20, 1989).
8. Torrey, 18, 21.
9. *Fasting* is not included in all translations. Actually, the textual evidence supporting the longer reading is quite strong. Without getting into a discussion of a very complex subject, I accept the longer reading as genuine. My view is based on Henry Sturz' thesis in *The Byzantine Text Type in New Testament Textual Criticism.*

Chapter 13
Confronting the Difficulties of Prayer

1. *Bits and Pieces,* Vol. I, No. 6. Published by Lawrence Ragan Communications, Inc., 316 N. Michigan Ave., Chicago, IL 60601.

2. *Alpha* and *omega* are the first and last letters of the Greek alphabet.

3. We are more conscious of this at the turn of a new century than ever before in human history. The globe is staggering under the curse of sinful, wasteful, thoughtless, shortsighted humankind. Howard Snyder, in his book *Foresight: Ten Major Trends that Will Dramatically Affect the Future of Christians and the Church,* lists as one of those trends moving "from threatened nations to threatened planet."

4. Romans 8:26 is thought by many to be a reference to speaking in tongues, or *glossolalia.* I disagree. It is quite clear that the groanings of the Spirit are not expressible in words. They cannot be uttered. Speaking in tongues may sound like groaning, but it is groaning that can be expressed and heard. The groaning of the Spirit is silent to the human ears, just like the other "groanings" to which Paul refers in this passage (see verses 22-23). Furthermore, the Greek preposition *huper,* used twice by itself in verses 26 [variant reading] and 27 and once in the compound verb *huperentuchano* (verse 26), means "over" or "in behalf of." Speaking in tongues is the Holy Spirit praying *in* us and *through* us, not *over* us. I believe that speaking in tongues is a valid gift in the church today (see my first book *And Signs Shall Follow*) but what we believe about tongues must be based on passages other than Romans 8:26. Speaking in tongues is not unrelated, however,

to the intercession of the Spirit, because it is a wonderful spiritual exercise when you do not know what to pray or how to pray.

5. This is not the Joshua who fought the battle of Jericho.

Chapter 14
The Kingdom Power of Praise

1. Aramaic, a kind of Hebrew dialect, was the common language spoken by Jesus and His disciples.
2. Ron Ford, "The Powerful Advance of God's Kingdom in the Earth," *First Fruits* (January/February 1986), 16.

Index

Scriptural Index

Genesis
   1:26-27, 63, 64, 65
   2:7, 86
   3:8-13, 35
     15, 69
   4:1 ff., 35

Exodus
   32:24, 36

Leviticus
   26:7-8, 28

Deuteronomy
   6:4, 63

2 Kings
   6:8-22, 88

2 Chronicles
   20:1 ff., 168

Psalms
   2:7, 107
   8:2, 166
     4-6, 167